WITH BOMBER COMMAND

The Story of Warrant Officer John Colin Sedgley

(11th January 1920 - 6th March 1995)

John C. Sedgley
West Bromwich Local History Society
ISBN 978-1-5272-2351-6

Dedication and introduction

This story is dedicated to the memory of the men and women of World War Two Bomber Command 1939-1945 who, despite the odds and the price being paid, continued with great courage to take the fight to Hitler's Germany. The damage they inflicted on the enemy played a major part in achieving the final defeat of the Nazi regime. Of the 125,000 aircrew that took part from 3rd September 1939 to 8th May 1945, the following were killed in action, accidents or their fates are still unknown to this day: -

Royal Air Force	39,589
Royal Australian Air Force	4,089
Royal Canadian Air Force	10,148
Royal New Zealand Air Force	1,699
Polish Air Force	960
Free French Air Force	218
Royal Indian Air Force	4
Royal Norwegian Air Force	35
South African Air Force	11
Women's Auxiliary Air Force	36
Total	56,789

In addition, a total of 138 attached personnel (including 68 members of the United States Air Force) also lost their lives, making a total of 56,927. A further 8,403 were wounded and 9,838 were prisoners of war. This gives a total number of killed, wounded and imprisoned of 75,168, which was 60 percent of the total force. This figure is one of the highest, if not the highest, of all the forces taking part in the Second World War.

The statistical summary of bomber command operations are: -

Total sorties:	392,137
Total bombs dropped:	955,044 tons
Total aircraft lost:	12,330
Total mines laid:	47,307
Victoria Crosses awarded:	19

If we consider the fighter pilots who won the Battle of Britain during 1940 to be the first coming of 'The Few', then surely the pilots and aircrew of Bomber Command may be thought of as the second coming of 'The

2

Few'. (*Never in the field of human conflict was so much owed by so many to so few*' was the famous line from a wartime speech by Prime Minister Winston Churchill on August 20th, 1940, referring to the ongoing efforts of the Royal Air Force crews defending Britain.)

At the end of the war, Churchill wrote the following to the Bomber Command leader Sir Arthur Harris (who was popularly known as 'Bomber Harris'):

> *'All your operations were planned with great care and skill, they were executed in the face of desperate opposition and appalling hazards, they made a decisive contribution to Germany's final defeat. The conduct of the operations demonstrated the fiery gallant spirit which animated your aircrews and the high sense of duty of all ranks under your command. I believe that the massive achievements of Bomber Command will long be remembered as an example of duty nobly done.'*

John's early life

I believe every one of the 125,000 who served would have a story to tell, a story of triumphs and tragedies, great happiness and great sadness, great modesty in telling their story and great pride in doing their duty. They may have talked of the bravery of their comrades but never the bravery of themselves.

The story I am about to tell will details the life of just one of these aircrew, along with the inclusion of small parts of the stories of some of his fellow airmen.

John was born in West Bromwich on the 11th January, 1920; he was the second son of Harold Sedgley and Nellie Sedgley, née Rogers, Harold's ancestors having lived in the town for many generations while those of Nellie came from Barry Town, South Wales.

John had five brothers and six sisters - one of whom, Joyce Muriel, died at only 9 months. Two of his brothers also served their country during World War Two, Arthur in the Royal Engineers and Albert in the Royal Navy. His sister Rosa also served as a driver in the auxiliary transport service, her duties were to transport supplies across Europe after the 1944 Normandy invasion. His siblings were all born between February 1915 and November 1937, one every two years.

John was known to his family, friends and his comrades in Bomber Command as Colin or Col, so I will therefore refer to him as such throughout

3

this story. No-one I have spoken to within the family seem to know why his second Christian name was adopted.

History will confirm that life was tough during the 1920s and 1930s; however, Colin was a very bright boy and after leaving Lyng junior school he attended West Bromwich municipal secondary school, which was based at the West Bromwich Institute on Lodge Road. When he attended during the early 1930s all the pupils were West Bromwich children. This school was formed in 1902, helped by a donation made by Sir George Kenrick; it was extended in the years 1907 and 1909 and during reorganisation in 1944 it became the only Grammar School in the town. In 1964 the school moved to new premises in Clarkes Lane, changing its name to Menzies High School in 1969. In 2010, the school merged with Manor High School and became the Phoenix Collegiate.

On leaving school Colin had a very brief employment at Accles and Pollock in Oldbury before securing a position at the newly formed group of companies known as Birmid Industries based in Smethwick. They produced castings for many industries and were leaders in the field of magnesium casting. By 1937 Birmid consisted of the following companies: Birmingham Aluminium Casting Co.; Midland Motor Cylinder Co.; Sterling Metals; Pneulec; Dartmouth Auto Castings; Exeloid Co.; Birmabright; Birmetals.

Colin was employed by Midland Motor Cylinder in the production management department.

Joining the Brylcream Boys

The above term was a nickname given to RAF aircrew. They were always smartly dressed with not a hair out of place, with a clearly defined parting plastered down using Brylcream - which was a white cream made up of water, mineral oil and beeswax. Having used it in my youth I remember it to be messy and it left a stain wherever you rested your head.

War with Germany broke out on 3rd September 1939, with British forces being despatched to France. With the disaster of the Dunkirk evacuation, 26th May - 4th June 1940, and the subsequent Battle of Britain from July to October 1940, the government was calling up all fit and able men to fight for their country's survival. The Battle of Britain saw a greatly outnumbered force of RAF fighter pilots win a decisive victory over the German Luftwaffe, with the following losses: -

RAF aircrew	1,542 killed
Aircraft destroyed	1,744
Luftwaffe aircrew	2,585 killed, 925 captured
Aircraft destroyed	1,977

Colin enlisted and volunteered for duty as aircrew on the 15th July 1940. Aircrew were in the main university graduates or Grammar School educated. They were all volunteers and there were no shortage of these, despite the low level life expectancy - for example, for a rear gunner on operations this was only three weeks.

Colin reported to RAF Cardington, located in Bedfordshire, for his induction. Cardington was originally an airship base and even today the massive hangars are preserved, although the base is no longer in use. After swearing allegiance to the Crown and answering a roll call giving his name and religion he was given the official number 1172570, an ID card and ID discs (known as dog tags) and the rank of Aircraftman Second Class (A.C.2). His record tells us that his height is 5' 9$3/4$, chest 32$1/2$', his hair fair and eyes grey. After this he was held on reserve awaiting his first posting for training.

Training begins

Colin was posted to No. 10 Signals recruit centre at Blackpool, where he arrived on 23rd August 1940. This centre later became 13 Radio School. His initial training was for a period of three months and included a fitness regime with lots of P.T. on the seashore, drill and games with the aim of becoming the best of the armed services. It was back to school, learning

Morse code, Aldis lamp and flag communications and the limitations of communicating by Morse and voice. Morse code was taught at the Winter Gardens with lectures and other tuition taking place in the Tower Ballroom, in short every facility that was available was used. Tests were carried out in upstairs rooms of Burton the tailors, with the minimum requirement being the ability to send and receive Morse at 12 words per minute. They also received firearms training at a nearby range.

The men were organised in squads of 50, each with a NCO instructor with the rank of corporal or sergeant. The next senior officer was usually a flight sergeant with a pilot officer as commanding officer of the squadron. A squadron had 10 squads of 50 men, making a total of 500.

These squadrons were given prefixes of A, B, C, etcetera. Squadrons were part of Wings, again with prefixes 1, 2, 3, etcetera. Each Wing had a commanding officer such as a squadron leader, an adjutant and a padre. At its peak 10,000 plus men were being trained at Blackpool, with the men billeted all over the town in hotels and guest-houses.

There was great friendship and comradeship in the squads and intense competition between squads to be the best, which led to a high level of discipline and drill. There was good humour with frequent sing songs and joviality when appropriate but, when needed, a seriousness and determination to learn the skills required to become good airmen. They knew even at this stage of their training that the average life of an airman flying over Germany was only 12 weeks and that many of them would undoubtedly die for their country.

RAF Yatesbury

Having achieved the necessary standard, on 22nd November 1940 Colin was posted to No. 2 Signals School at RAF Yatesbury in the county of Wiltshire. The base was about four miles east of the town of Calne. (It closed in 1965 - only derelict buildings remain.) Here the physical training and wireless training continued with Colin qualifying on 12th February 1941 as an A.C.2 wireless operator. His Morse speed was 18 words per minute send and receive, this speed just above the minimum requirement. His first training flight had taken place a month before, on 28th December 1940, with a Mr. O'Conner, for a duration of 30 minutes; the purpose of the flight was to tune the radio for receiving signals. His second flight, of one hour, was on 17th January 1941, with a Mr. Horuidge, to tune the radio for transmitting signals. The aircraft used was a de Havilland

Dragon Rapide Mk I, referred to in the service as a Dominie, an elegant biplane used for training and also as an air ambulance by the RAF and the Fleet Air Arm. It was powered by two 150 kw Gipsy Queen engines, which gave it a maximum speed of 250 kilometres per hour, a ceiling of 16,000 feet and a range of 920 kilometres. It had a crew of two - pilot and wireless operator/navigator.

Dominie Mk II © IWM (CH 14714).

RAF Honington

Colin was now posted to RAF Honington in Suffolk on 15th February 1941. His status was 'headquarters holding'; this meant he was supernumerary to the complement of the station, awaiting posting for further training. While it was the responsibility of the commanding officer of RAF Honington to ensure all such men posted to his station maintained their fitness and training and were fully equipped, he could not post these men as they were 'owned' by headquarters. This holding of men was a normal occurrence at a time when thousands were being trained.

RAF Honington is still in use today as a training facility and a base for RAF regiments. At the time Colin was there it was home base to IX Squadron who had, on 4th September 1939, carried out the first bombing raid of the war when they attacked the German fleet at Wilhelmshaven and Brunsbüttel, at the entrance to the Kiel Canal. It was also home base to 311 Squadron (Czech) and several other units. Later in 1942 the station was handed to the United States 8th Army Air Force, returning to the RAF in 1946. During the Cold War it was one of the main V-weapon bases with Valliant and Victor aircraft. RAF Honington is situated between the towns of Bury St. Edmunds to the south and Thetford to the north.

Hangar, RAF Yatesbury, Wiltshire. (Photograph by Vieve Forward, 2014, CC BY-SA 2.0).

Return to RAF Yatesbury

Colin was soon posted back to No. 2 Signals School on 29th August 1941, where he was now subjected to two weeks intensive wireless operator training - which included the dreaded Harwell Box or, as the trainees called it, 'the Horrible Box'.

The box was designed at RAF station Harwell (hence the name) during 1940 to simulate flying conditions on the ground. It was a small wooden box comparable with the accommodation the trainee would have in an aircraft, fitted with all the appropriate radio equipment. Signals were fed to his radio set simulating airborne conditions; in addition a loudspeaker would bombard him with aircraft engine noise and intermittent bursts of machine gun fire. One model of the box included a method of moving the box simulating movements he would experience in flight. All this was attempted in full flying kit and an oxygen mask if the instructor so wished. They were poorly lit and badly ventilated, ensuring that without the cooling effect of flying at several thousand feet the trainees were hot and sweaty and very glad when the exercise was over.

As well as ground exercises they also did flying exercises for a total of 8 hours; these included frequency changing, Rx and Tx tuning, Bk tuning and df loop direction finding, this in particular was a boon to navigation which did not advertise the position of the aircraft to enemy wireless operators. The training also included fault finding, coil changing and G messaging - G or Gee was an early radar navigational system, the successful trials of this being carried out by 115 Squadron during August 1941.

Apart from the Dominie, Colin also trained in the Percival Proctor Mk II, a radio and communications trainer. It was a three-seater duel control aircraft powered by one 210 hp engine.

Percival Proctor III, Imperial War Museum, Duxford.
(Photograph by Przemysław Jahr.)

Air Gunner training

Colin's next posting on 26th September 1941 was to No. 5 Air Observer School at RAF Jurby, in the north west of the Isle of Man. Jurby also was home to five fighter squadrons whose main job was to protect Belfast and Liverpool from German air raids. He had now been promoted to leading aircraftsman effective from 28th September. Here trainees undertook armament, bombing, gunnery and navigation training. He immediately commenced his gunnery training, the aircraft used was a Bristol Blenheim Mk I with a crew of three - pilot, navigator; bombardier and wireless operator; air gunner. Powered by two Bristol Mercury engines, each producing 860 hp. Its armament consisted of a single forward firing .303 Browning machine gun and a turreted .303 Vickers machine gun firing to the rear. It had a maximum speed of 266 mph a range of 1,460 miles and a ceiling height of 27,260 feet. It could also carry a 1,000lb bomb in its bomb bay.

Ground firing was carried out with a .303 browning machine gun and from a Frazer-Nash turret, a hydraulically operated turret fitted to Wellington bombers. Ground training also included gun cleaning, harmonisation, range estimation and aircraft recognition. Air firing was practised on 'drogues' towed behind single-engine aircraft adapted for the purpose, such as the Westland Wallace and Hawker Henleys.

Colin's training included 12 hours 15 minutes flying and firing over 2,000 rounds of ammunition, after which he qualified as Air Gunner achieving an examination score of 72.4% with final remarks of 'a good average air gunner, possible bomb aimer'. He qualified as Air Gunner on 8th November 1941, with his rank now being sergeant.

Bristol Blenheim bomber © IWM (CH 364).

Operational Training Unit 27

RAF Litchfield was also known as Fradley aerodrome and was situated two miles north east of Litchfield, Staffordshire. It is now known as Fradley Park with industrial units and houses built there; however almost all of the hangers still exist, with the majority having been refurbished to be used for industrial purposes. It became an OPU (operational training unit) during 1941, its role to form and train aircrew for bombing operations using, when Colin was there, Wellington bombers. The crews were largely from Commonwealth countries, such as Canada, Australia and New Zealand. After training, the crew were then posted to their squadrons, mostly in Lincolnshire. Colin arrived in Litchfield on 18th November 1941, with his flying training commencing on 26th January 1942.

The new intake of airmen at these units were paraded in a hangar and told to form themselves into five man crews of pilot, navigator, wireless operator, bomb aimer and an air gunner. Most were happy to crew up like this - however if they failed to form into a good team due to incompatibility, they split up and tried other crews. It was not unknown for some to try several crews until they were happy.

The pilot was captain of the aircraft regardless of his rank; he could be a sergeant with a pilot officer in his crew and when flying a first name policy was adopted. The comradeship of crews was such that they felt they were all in it together and stuck together during socialising periods off duty regardless of rank. One example of such comradeship occurred at a local pub when dozens of aircrew arrived and the sergeants and flight sergeants were refused service in the lounge bar, being told this room was for officers only and that NCO's would only be served in the public bar. They obeyed this rule made by a new barmaid and departed into the public bar. The officers all left their pints in the lounge and followed into the bar. The rule was soon rescinded. Any member of aircrew at any time could decline to fly on further operations, but these men were immediately branded as lacking in moral fibre, de-ranked, removed from their squadron and given menial tasks.

By the time flying training began in earnest on 26th January 1942 Colin had clocked up 22 hours and 5 minutes of flying time. By the end of February this had increased to 38 hours, 55 minutes - 2 hours and 30 minutes of this night flying. All but 50 minutes of this time took place in Avro Anson aircraft. Those used for training purposes were fitted with dual controls and usually had the gun turret removed, although those used for gunnery training were fitted with a gun turret similar to that used in the Bristol Blenheim. The Anson was powered by two Armstrong Siddeley engines, rated at 350 hp each. The Anson had a four-man crew.

Their training was mainly cross-country flying, testing navigational skills and wireless telegraphy, with a typical flight from base to Luton, Norwich, Northampton and back to base. Seven different pilots carried out these training flights, ranging in rank from sergeant to flight lieutenant.

Most instructors were airmen who had carried out at least one tour of operations duty. One tour of duty was 30 completed operations where the first or secondary target had been attacked successfully. After 6 months as instructors they would go back to operations and do a further tour of 20 operations. After this, if they survived, they could volunteer for more missions or remain as instructors.

Avro Anson. (Photograph by Oren Rozen, CC BY-SA 3.0).

The final flight of 50 minutes was Colin's first recorded flight in a Wellington bomber. It consisted of wireless telegraphy exercises, with takeoffs, circuits of the base and landings, presumably to familiarise the crews with the working of the aircraft.

During March 1942 Colin continued training with day flying time of 14 hours and 50 minutes, but now in a Wellington; his duty on these flights was as first wireless operator. The training consisted of the usual circuits and landings, a 2 hour and 30 minute flight, flying on one engine and an altitude test of 2 hours duration at a height of 15,000 feet using oxygen, not very pleasant with an outside temperature of minus 12 degrees centigrade. These aircraft did not have pressurised oxygenated cabins with heating and only had a fabric outer skin.

During his training he had become friends with many of his comrades, one in particular was John Francis Garland, a New Zealander, RNZAF No. 403440. They became firm friends and, with aircrew receiving one week's leave every six weeks, Colin and John would frequently spend their leave together at 47 Lyng Lane, West Bromwich. They also visited Colin's elder brother Harold, living in Carters Green, and had many eat, drink and be merry nights for tomorrow we may die. Harold was my father, who was bitterly disappointed he could not serve, having failed the medical mainly due to his poor eyesight.

John and Colin, 19th March 1942.

I can remember my mother telling me the mushroom story. It goes like this. The boys, as she called John and Colin, enquired where they could buy mushrooms as they had a great desire for the taste. My mother told them she had not seen mushrooms for some time. Undeterred, the boys left for the Golden Mile (what West Bromwich high street was locally known as at that time). They arrived back, several pints later, in triumph with a bag. On opening the bag my mother exclaimed, 'You can't eat these, there are more maggots than mushrooms.' The boys had a quick look and said, 'Cook them.' The maggotty mushrooms were duly cooked and the boys ate the lot, with great appetite and relish, maggots and all then left on their merry way.

In December 1942, John was a member of 115 Squadron (motto 'Despite the Elements') based at East Wretham, six miles north east of Thetford in Norfolk. It closed as an air base in 1946. His rank at this time was flight sergeant and he was a qualified wireless operator/airgunner.

On 3rd December 1942, his Wellington Mk III, code No. bk338, took off at 11.41 pm to attack Frankfurt. Unfortunately, out of 112 aircraft his aircraft was one of the seven which did not return to base. The incident, which caused the loss of his aircraft, is unknown to this day. By the end of the war the crew were reported as missing, presumed killed.

Below is a transcript of a letter from his mother to Colin's parents, dated 28th April 1945.

6, Fife Lane,
Wiseman,
Wellington,
New Zealand

Dear Mr and Mrs Sedgley
I received your letter after a long delay in transit.
I want to thank you sincerely for all you did for my son John, when the
mails are more certain I will write you a letter stating our feelings more fully.
We are still hoping we may yet hear our boy is somewhere alive.
We hope to return to England after this war is over, if so I will call on you
and thank you personally for your great kindness. Please kiss baby John for me,
I pray he may be just a fine a son as mine when he grows up.
God bless you and yours.

Yours sincerely,
Brenda Garland

Brenda and her husband William had emigrated to New Zealand some years earlier. I do not know if they ever returned or had further contact with my grandparents. I am the baby John mentioned.

Their hope that their son John may yet turn up was not to be. During late 1945 and early 1946 the bodies of mainly airmen were recovered from numerous German cemeteries and reinterred at Rheinberg war cemetery, which was created for this purpose. 3,330 are buried there, of which 158 are unidentified.

It was discovered that John's aircraft had crashed near Monzernheim, 14 kilometres north-west of Worms in Germany's Rhineland - which is now the centre of Germany's wine growing district. All the crew had been killed and buried at the local cemetery. From the location of the crash they could have been either approaching or leaving the target city of Frankfurt.

Wellington Mk III, 115 Squadron Bomber © IWM (CH 166994).

The rest of John's crew were:
- RCAF, Athol, Malver, William, McCrae, warrant officer second class service No. r/93497 pilot and therefore captain of the aircraft.
- RCAF, Albert, Morse, Borden, Johnson, flight sergeant service No. r/84820 observer - observers did several duties such as navigator, bomb aimer and even air gunner.
- RCAF Joseph, Cecil, Swarbrick, flight sergeant service No. r/77417 warrant officer second class - air gunner on this mission.
- RCAF Eugene, Simbalist, flight sergeant service No. r/76610, observer.

John was just 21 years old at the time of his death but had recorded 396 flying hours and was carrying out his 32nd operation against the enemy.

Colin was selected for bomb aimer's training, which continued during April 1942 with map reading and bombing runs over Cannock Chase bombing range. This is a 68-acre area with heathland, wooded areas and lakes, with wild life including red and roe deer. It is also home to Britain's only poisonous snake, the adder. It is used today for recreational purposes such as cycling and walking, with the woodland managed by the Forestry Commission. Several different pilots were used on these flights with Anson and Wellington aircraft being utilised. His flying time during April was 21 hours and 40 minutes.

From 4th May until 21st May 1942 the training intensified with 17 hours daylight flying and 30 hours and 5 minutes night flying, with bombs being dropped at the Cannock range night and day. During these bombing runs Colin was, as you would expect, in control of the aircraft. Wellingtons were the aircraft used on all these flights.

Squadron leader Richard (Dick) Collard took one of the flights and put the crew through its paces with Colin as bomb aimer and front gunner with air firing and simulation bombing. It was usual for the bomb aimer and front gunner duties to be combined. Most of the other flights were piloted by sergeant Isaacson.

On 21st May 1942, Colin qualified with a proficiency assessment of 'above average' as a bombardier.

The Wellington bomber

The Vickers Wellington was designed by Barnes Wallis, later of the Dam Busters bomb fame, in the early 1930s. The air-frame was of a duralumin; this is a trade name for an age hardening aluminium alloy with typically 4% copper and 0.5% magnesium and manganese, developed ironically by the German metallurgist Alfred Wilm. When hardened this material was light and strong. A basket weave construction was used with a skin of doped fabric - this was a plasticised lacquer which tightened and stiffened fabric stretched over airframes, rendering them airtight and weatherproof.

The Wellington Mk II, in which all of Colin's operations were flown, was powered by two Rolls Royce Merlin xv12 engines, each producing 1,145hp. The aircraft was 65 feet long, with a width of 86 feet (including wing span) and stood at its highest 16 feet from the ground. It had a maximum speed of 255 mph, a range of 1,540 miles, a maximum height of 19,000 feet and could carry 4,500 lbs of bombs. It also had two hydraulic operated Frazer Nash 5 gun turrets, the front and rear both mounted with two Browning

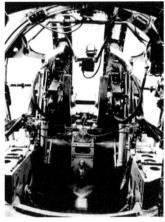

Left: Despite severe damage, the unique basket weave design enabled this particular plane to safely land. © IWM(CH 9867).

Right: Looking into rear turret from fuselage.

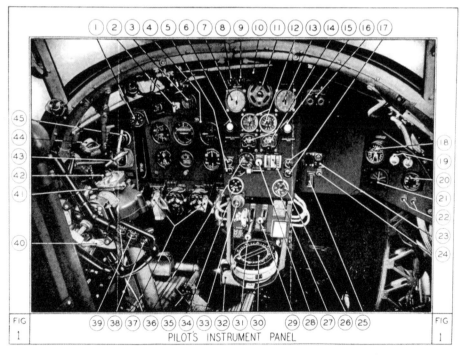

View of cockpit, from World War Two training manual.

Mk II .303 machine guns. The rear guns fired 2,000 rpm per gun with the front 1,000 rpm per gun. The guns were located either side of the gunner with easy access in case of blockage or other problems. The guns were fed by ammunition cases on either side, which were also used by the gunner as armrests. In operation the rear turret had no effect on the aircraft; however, the front, when fully turned to one side, caused vibration and affected the flight characteristics.

To abandon the aircraft, the rear gunner would turn the turret to one side open the rear door and fall out. The front gunner was not so fortunate; firstly there was not enough room within the turret for him to wear his parachute, so this was hung on a hook inside the fuselage. To abandon the aircraft the gunner would have to ensure the turret was pointing forward, open the rear door and grab his parachute, somehow put it on and exit through the bomb aimer hatch or the escape push out panel on the side of the aircraft. If the turret was partly turned and jammed due to enemy action the gunner was trapped; if he could open the rear door he could risk exiting past the spinning propeller; but if this was his only choice it was better than staying in the crashing aircraft, though he would know his chances of avoiding the propeller were very slim.

The bomb aimer lay prone on a Perspex window at the nose of the aircraft with only his bombsight for company. The aircraft usually had a crew of five.

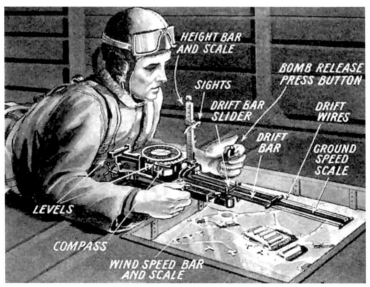

Bomb aimer in bombing position, from World War Two manual.

Operations

Colin was now posted along with, I believe, the rest of the crew he had trained with when qualifying as a bombardier, the pilot being sergeant Isaacson to No. 26 operational training unit. This unit was based at RAF Wing, a bomber training station located in the Aylesbury Vale district of Buckinghamshire, with a nearby satellite station RAF Cheddington. Colin and the rest of the crew arrived at Cheddington on 25/26th May 1942.

On 27th May they flew Wellington dv 721 to RAF Graveley, five miles south of Huntington in Cambridgeshire. At this time aircraft were being dispersed to airfields in eastern England in preparation for the first 'thousand-bomber raid' on Germany. Colin and the rest of the crew now knew that their first operation against the enemy would be this particular raid, the first of its kind in warfare. The term was a propaganda device to show the growing strength of the RAF; there were actually a total of 1,047 aircraft involved and it was code-named 'Operation Millenium'.

On 29th May, with Colin as bomb aimer, the crew air tested the Wellington to ensure all systems and equipment operated correctly. With weather conditions being favourable, the raid took place the very next night. Their target was the city of Cologne.

Aircraft taking part were:

602 Wellingtons
131 Halifaxes
88 Stirlings
29 Hamptons
73 Lancasters
46 Manchesters
28 Whitleys

Wellington dv 721, with Colin as the bomb aimer, took off at 22.45 hours on 30th May for the 5 hour round trip flight. Three 500 lb general purpose bombs and six small bomb containers, each loaded with 30 lb incendiaries, were dropped. The general-purpose bombs were either fitted with delay or instantaneous fuses.

This was the first time the 'bomber stream' tactic was used, whereby all aircraft flew a common route at a given height and speed in a time slot, thus minimising the risk of mid-air collision. (Of 41 planes lost during this operation, only 2 were actually due to collision.) With the early radar system Gee also being used it was easier for the crews to navigate within the precise limits required for such flying. Gee worked by measuring the time delay between two radio signals to produce a fix with accuracy of a few hundred feet and an updated version is still used today.

To make up the 1,047 aircraft it was necessary use crews who were not yet fully trained, such as Colins. This proved effective in that casualties in this group were no higher than the fully trained aircrews. The raid was a great success. Two and a half thousand separate fires were started with 1,700 classed by the German fire brigades as 'large'. Some 12,840 buildings were damaged. Many factories suffered complete loss of production. It also brought home to the Germans that they were at last on the receiving end of the terror they had inflicted on so many others.

Wellington dv 721 landed back at RAF Oakington, five miles north west of Cambridge at approximately 03.45 hours with little damage sustained. Later that day, they returned to RAF Gravely, then the crew air tested their aircraft on the afternoon of 1st June and prepared for the second 'thousand-bomber raid' that night on the city of Essen. The number of bombers involved in this operation was actually 956, all that could be assembled at the time.

Colin was again bomb aimer on this flight, taking off at 23.05 hours and returning to RAF Gravely at 03.50 hours having dropped one 500lb general purpose bomb and six small bomb containers loaded with 4lb incendiaries. Sustaining little damage to the aircraft, they returned to RAF Cheddington. This second raid was not so successful, with little damage caused. This was the last flight Colin was to make in this particular aircraft. He had now clocked up 93.3 hours daylight flying time and 32.35 hours of night flying.

These raids gave Bomber Command and the country a great lift in morale, a demonstration of air power with acceptable losses; it also gave the commander of Bomber Command, Arthur Harris, his nickname as 'Bomber Harris' and placed him firmly in the public eye.

After a short leave, on 12th June Colin was posted to 460 Squadron based at RAF Breighton in the East Riding of Yorkshire on the bank of the river Derwent, five miles north-west of Howden. It is still in use today, housing historic aircraft and hosting air shows.

460 Squadron's aircrew were mainly Australian and were formed from C flight of RAAF 458 Squadron; they dropped more tonnage of bombs than any other squadron of Bomber Command. His duties whilst at this posting are not known. From his flying logbook he did not have any flights during the short time he was there, which was only until 20th June.

12 Squadron

Colin was now posted to 12 Squadron at RAF Binbrook, Lincolnshire, arriving there on 21st June 1942. Their motto was 'Leads the Field'. They were part of No. 1 Group, whose motto was 'Swift to Attack'. (The airfield was later used as the location for filming of the 1990 film 'Memphis Belle', the story of an American bomber's last mission of its tour of duty.) Here he made up a new crew, with pilot officer Morton as pilot. Now came 5 hours of flying day and night familiarising the crew with each other with Colin as bomb aimer, in preparation of the third and last 1,000 bomber raid, the target Bremen. This took place on 25th June, with 1,067 aircraft taking part. His plane, Wellington 1341, took off at 23.15 hours and returned safely at 04.45 having dropped 9 bomb containers carrying 4 lb incendiaries.

The aircraft on which he had carried out the first two raids, Wellington dv 721, was also involved in this operation and shot down. The crew all died and were interred at Kiel cemetery in north Germany.

They were:

f/sgt. D.H. Baddeley RAF pilot

f/o A. Sharpes RAF

w/o C.J. Stirling RNZAF

f/s H.H. Jordan RAF

f/s A.R. Watkins RAF

On this third raid the losses of training crews were considered higher than acceptable, so the use of so many such crews was then curtailed - if used in further raids they were in much lower numbers.

On 26th June Wellington 1315, with Colin now as front gunner, took off at 23.30 hours and returned safely at 03.15 hours having laid two 1,000 lb mines off Terschelling Island, one of a string of islands off the Netherland coast. The nearest large mainland town was Leeuwarden.

At the end of June, in Wellington 8644 Colin did circuits and landings, practicing wireless operation and rear gunner duties. He had now clocked up 96 hours 20 minutes daylight and 42 hours 20 minutes night flying.

The first two days of July were taken up with more practice as bomb aimer and front gunner. On the night of 2nd July Wellington 8356, with Colin as rear gunner, took off at 23.30 hours and returned safely at 04.25 hours, having dropped 9 small bomb containers carrying 4 lb incendiaries on the city of Bremen. On 8th July, 1942 Wellington 8648, with Colin again as rear gunner, took off at 23.50 hours and returned safely (but damaged) at

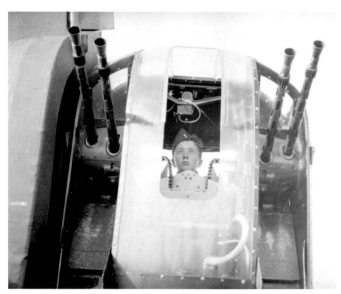

Rear turret showing four guns instead of two; these Frazer Nash 20 turrets were first fitted to Wellington Mk III aircraft. © IWM (CH 13880).

04.10 hours, having dropped a 4,000 lb high explosive bomb on the port of Wilhelmshaven in Lower Saxony, north of Bremen.

His logbook report is as follows: -

· *Engaged by enemy aircraft a j.u.88. Fired four bursts, enemy aircraft broke off engagement, own aircraft hit by cannon and machine gun fire, pilot (pilot officer Morton) wounded in leg, turrets u/s. Hapless landing at base.*

It was general practice with aircrews that the pilot unofficially trained one of the crew to fly the aircraft in an emergency. With pilot officer Morton drifting in and out of consciousness, Colin took over the controls and flew the crippled aircraft back to base. He was not yet a fully trained pilot (but had the ambition to be one) so he could not land the aircraft. He said these immortal words to his crewmates: 'Bring him (the pilot) round because I can't land this bloody thing!' or words to that effect. Morton took over the controls and, although not a textbook landing, put the aircraft down to the relief of all the crew.

The enemy's Junker Ju 88 was a formidable and very versatile fighter bomber with different models. One such version was the Ju 88c series night fighter; this aircraft had a crew of three or four with an armament consisting of two 7.9mm machine guns and one 20mm cannon mounted in the nose and one 7.9mm machine gun mounted at the rear. It was faster and able to manoeuvre quicker than the Wellington. I believe that, considering the above, the only reason it broke off its attack on Colin's plane was due to the returning fire from his front gunner crewmate.

Colin's aspiration to be a pilot was now to be realised with a posting to a fighter squadron, which took place in late August/early September. However, before this he had his seventh operational bombing mission to carry out on 25th July. The mission was to attack the city of Duisburg, located in Lower Rhineland, at the confluence of the Rhine and Ruhr rivers. The city had the largest inland harbour in the world and was renowned for steel making.

Due to aircraft and aircrew losses, the pilot on this flight was the Station Commander of 12 Squadron, wing commander Richard (Dick) Collard. Colin's duty on this flight was front gunner/bombardier.

Wellington z8591 took off at 23.59 hours, the anti-aircraft fire over the target (known as flak) was particularly heavy, damaging their aircraft. 313 planes were used in this raid, with 12 losses - 7 Wellingtons, 2 Halifaxes, 2 Lancasters and 1 Stirling. The German anti-aircraft shells were fired from ground based artillery guns with fuses designed to explode the shells at a certain height as the aircraft passed overhead. These proved very effective

Junkers Ju 88c Night Fighter, Air Ministry Air Diagram,
published March 1944.

in damaging and downing aircraft. Thick cloud also covered the target, making the raid less effective.

Having made its bombing run, z8591 turned and made for home. However, even with the exception flying skill of wing commander Collard, control of the aircraft was slowly being lost. At 2.30 hours he instructed the crew to bail out.

Collard held the aircraft as steady as possible, as the crew bailed out. I believe that Colin, after donning his parachute, would have likely used the emergency hatch at the rear of the fuselage, this being much safer than using the front turret. He felt relief when his parachute opened (many failed) and he drifted almost silently towards the ground, which he could not see in the dark. He descended not knowing that his dream of becoming a pilot was not now to be realised, nor that he would not see home again for almost three years.

He twisted his leg on landing, in a field somewhere in Holland. The injury was not serious and he quickly unclipped his parachute and buried it. All aircrew were given instruction on evasion, issued with local money, a compass, a silk map and an aid box containing enough food to sustain them for 48 hours. I am not sure if he had these items with him, as I cannot recall any mention of them in conversations with him.

However, as he chose a direction and set off, it soon became clear to him he was in farming country with level terrain and few buildings. After about an hours walk, as it became lighter, he saw a farmhouse and decided to approach it. Arriving at the farm at about 04.00 hours and feeling tired, he slept for about thirty minutes on a bench at the side of the farmhouse.

Upon waking he knocked on the farmhouse door; the door was opened by the farmer and Colin asked him for help. He was immediately invited in and looked after by the farmer, who then dispatched his son to inform the local resistance leader of Colin's presence. In due course a member of the resistance arrived with civilian clothes for him to change into, his RAF uniform being disposed of.

It was Sunday 26th July; about noon that day he was taken by the resistance man to a nearby wood where he was told to hide until midnight when his escort for the next stage of the journey to return him to England would arrive, whistling the British national anthem to identify himself. In good spirits, knowing he was in the hands of the Dutch resistance, he had high hopes of returning home and waited patiently. At approximately 19.00 hours he heard a noise and was suddenly confronted by a patrol of

6 German soldiers who knew his exact hiding place. He was now taken prisoner, betrayed by a traitor in the resistance.

He was transported to, as were all captured aircrew, the Dulag transit camp near to the city of Frankfurt for interrogation. There he was interrogated for three weeks; what that interrogation consisted of he never spoke of, but he knew that the lives of the farmer and his family were in his hands - if he talked they would be executed. Whatever story he told his interrogators is unknown, but suffice to say that farmer never had a visit from the Germans throughout the occupation of his country.

As for the fate of the rest of his crew: Sergeant G.D. Pepper was imprisoned in Stalag VIII-B Lamsdorf in Silesia (today called Łambinowice in Poland). I believe he survived his imprisonment and returned home. Flight lieutenant N. Thom RCAF, who broke his ankle during his parachute landing, was imprisoned in several camps including Stalag Luft III in Lower Silesia near the town of Sagan (now Żagań, Poland). Again, I believe he survived the war.

The pilot, wing commander R.C. Collard, DSO, DFC, was the last man to leave the stricken aircraft by his escape hatch near to his own seat. He was imprisoned in Stalag Luft III. After the war he rejoined the RAF and commanded the Lancaster aircraft goodwill tour of the USA. He then became commander of RAF Stradishall in Suffolk, retiring from the RAF during 1953 as group captain operations coastal command. With an interest in politics he became a member of parliament for Central Norfolk in 1959, and died in 1962. He now has a road named after him in Kenley, Surrey near RAF station Kenley.

The final member of the crew was pilot officer (observer) John Wilfred Naden, RAF volunteer reserve. John was killed during his parachute drop, the exact circumstances are unknown but it is believed his parachute snagged on the crashing aircraft.

Colin was unaware at the time he had lost another airman who had become a close friend. John was 30 years old and is interred at Amersfoort cemetery, Holland. He is remembered in his hometown of Macclesfield on the war memorial and also on the roll of honour in the annexe to that memorial.

Their aircraft crashed between Bunschoten and the town of Nijkerk north of Amersfoort city, the area being mainly flat and rural. The crew who survived that night can attribute their survival to the skills of their pilot.

Prisoner of war - 26th July 1942 to 16th April 1945

After interrogation at Dulag transit camp Colin was transferred to Stalag Luft III near Sagan, some 160 kilometres southeast of Berlin. This was the famous camp were 'The Great Escape' was to take place in April 1944. 76 prisoners escaped, 50 later captured and shot dead, including the escape leader Squadron Leader Roger Bushell. (The story is told in the 1963 film 'The Great Escape', based on Paul Brickhill's 1950 book of the same name.)

At this time in 1943 the camp had become so overcrowded that about 1,000 men, mainly non-commissioned aircrew were transferred to Stalag VIII-B at Lamsdorf. The aircrew were separated from the rest of the camp by a separate compound forming a camp within a camp. This particular camp also held thousands of prisoners from many countries including Russians.

Colin, now prisoner No. 25079 arrived at Stalag VIII-B some time between late August and early October of 1942. I have not been able to ascertain accurately the date of his transfer from Lamsdorf but I am sure he was there before the end of 1942 because of the following scenario.

On 19th August the ill-fated operation 'Jubilee' took place, a raid on Dieppe in northern France. The plan was to take the port, hold it for several hours and gather intelligence. Due to not having enough supporting fire power the invasion force of 5,000 Canadians, 1,000 British and 50 Americans were trapped on the beaches by the German defenders with non of the objectives of the operation achieved. Within a few hours the raid was abandoned with the survivors removed from the beaches. Of the attacking troops 3,500 were killed, wounded or captured.

The captured men were mainly Canadian and imprisoned at Stalag VIII-B On searching a prisoner, the Germans had found orders that any German captured by the invading force was to be hand tied temporarily, a breach of the Geneva Convention on treatment of prisoners. Adolf Hitler demanded an apology from Winston Churchill, Winston refusing on the basis that the tying was only for a limited period.

On 4th October British commandos raided the channel island of Sark, during which they tied the hands of some German prisoners and later shot them. An angry Hitler demanded an apology, or he would hand tie all prisoners taken at Dieppe. With no reply from the British he ordered the approximately 1,400 prisoners to be hand tied. When this did not provoke any reply he ordered a further 1,000 British prisoners to be tied. The bulk of these prisoners were aircrew. The British replied by tying German prisoners of war held in England. While this only lasted a few weeks, this was not so in camps in Germany.

The hand tying commenced at Stalag VIII-B on 8th October. Prisoners were tied from early morning to late evening. This continued until 2nd December when the rope was changed to handcuffs connected by chain. After several months, with the camp guards fed up with the work involved in fitting and removing the handcuffs, they would just deliver the handcuffs to the camp huts and collect them later in the evening. By using a bully beef tin key, the handcuffs were easily opened by the prisoners, so they were only worn when inspections were about to occur or when German officers were around. Some of the prisoners, after being handcuffed and un-handcuffed would re-handcuff or un-handcuff and get in line again, thus prolonging the process; the guards never did seem to know this was going on. When this practice ended is unclear, some records say 12 months others give a precise date of 21st November 1943.

From Colin's letter home dated 6th June 1943, to his sister Nell, he mentions he is no longer chained and never wants to see a chain or piece of rope again, thus my conclusion he was in Stalag VIII-B when this practice of tying began.

I will give full transcripts of all his known letters from the camp still in existence in their date order.

At his home, 47 Lyng Lane, West Bromwich, a handwritten telegram arrived on the 27th July 1942. It said: 'Regret to inform you that your son Sgt. John Sedgley is missing as the result of air operations 25/26 July 1942. Letter follows.'

The first letter to arrive was from 12 Squadron RAF Binbrook, dated 26th July 1942. This letter stated:

'While I can give you no actual details of what occurred, we did receive a wireless transmission from the aircraft which said the crew might have to bale out over enemy territory. This message showed that the crew had plenty of time to act, and although I do not wish to raise your hopes unduly, we all regard it as a favourable sign. Our Commanding Officer, who was a most experienced pilot was your son's Captain.'

The second arrived dated 28th July 1942. Both still being readable are printed on the next two pages and are self-explanatory.

No.12 Squadron,
Royal Air Force,
Binbrook, Lincoln.

26th. July 1942

Dear Mr. Sedgley,

I am writing to offer you my deep sympathy in your anxiety for your son, Sgt. John Colin Sedgley, who was reported missing from an operational flight on the night of 25th/26th. July 1942.

On that night your son was flying as Bombardier of an aircraft which took off on a mission against the enemy, but which failed to return. While I can give you no actual details of what occurred, we did receive a wireless message from the aircraft which said that the crew might have to bale out over enemy territory. This message showed that the crew had plenty of time in which to act, and although I do not wish to raise your hopes unduly, we all regard it as a favourable sign. Our Commanding Officer who was a most experienced and skillful pilot, was your son's Captain. You will, of course, be notified as soon as any further news is received.

Your son's personal effects are being sent to the Royal Air Force Central Depository at Colnbrook, Slough, Bucks., who will be writing to you about them in due course.

We were all very shocked to hear the bad news, and all the Officers and men of this Squadron, with whom your son was well acquainted and most popular, wish to add their sympathy to my own.

Yours sincerely,

Squadron Leader,
Commanding,
No.12 Squadron.

Mr. H.Sedgley,
47 Lyng Lane,
West Bromwich,
Staffs.

28

Telephone No. : SPRINGWELL (GLOUCESTER)........042
Telegraphic Address :
    RECORDS TELEX, GLOUCESTER.
Any communications on the
subject of this letter should
be addressed to :
AIR OFFICER i/c RECORDS,
        Address as opposite,
and the following number
quoted :—
    Your Ref. :........ C7/1172570

RECORD OFFICE,

ROYAL AIR FORCE,

GLOUCESTER.

Date........26th July 1942........

[handwritten: Binbrook Lincolnshire / Date of Birth 11/1/1920]

Dear Sir,

            I regret to confirm that your son No.1172570
Sergeant John Colin SEDGLEY of No. 12 Squadron, Royal
Air Force, is missing, the aircraft of which he was
a wireless operator and air gunner having failed to
return to its base on the 25th July 1942 from an
operational flight.

            This does not necessarily mean that he is
killed or wounded. I will communicate with you again
immediately I have any further news and would be obliged
if you, on your part, would write to me should you hear
anything of your son from unofficial sources.

            May I assure you of the sympathy of the Royal
Air Force with you in your anxiety.

                            I am,
                                Dear Sir,
                                Your obedient Servant,

                                [signature]

                                Air Commodore,
                                Air Officer i/c Records,
                                ROYAL   AIR   FORCE.

H. Sedgley, Esq.,
47 Lyng Lane,
West Bromwich,
Staffordshire.

29

Nothing further was heard of Colin's fate until 16th August when a telegram was received at 47 Lyng Lane stating that a German broadcast on 15th August had mentioned that he was a prisoner of war but that 'this information should be accepted with reserve pending official confirmation.' The confirmation finally arrived on 13th September with the Red Cross quoting Berlin information that Colin was indeed a prisoner - the official letter is reproduced on the next page.

As you would imagine, this news was a great relief to his family, in particular his mother who had been worrying herself sick. His father, who had served as an infantryman during the First World War, showed less outward emotion, no doubt due to his war experiences of surviving, in particular, the battle of the Somme and of being gassed and buried alive whilst sheltering in a shell hole, but that's another story.

I remember him on many occasions saying those who served in the Second World War had it much easier than those of his generation in 1914-18. As his grandson I found this hard to accept at the time, but with age and greater knowledge, but thankfully no experience of all-out war, I now respect his opinion.

Colin's letters were from Stalag VIII-B (which became Stalag 344 at the end of December 1943). The original letters are held by his family, they are all written in pencil and are now very fragile. They are likely not all the letters he wrote but are the only ones I am aware of still in existence.

Letters sent to Colin whilst a prisoner, of which there were many, no longer exist. I believe it's enough to say he would have used them for other purposes.

Please note the date these letters were received would have been considerably later than the written date.

22nd August 1942
Dear Dad, Mother and family
I hope everyone at home is alright and keeping fit and happy. I am still in good health and quite comfortable and I am looking forward to a few letters from you soon I have met a lot of Birmingham boys here so I am not getting homesick in fact we are all cheerful.

With all my love to everyone,
Col

Telephone No. : SPRINGWELL (GLOUCESTER) 2047.

Telegraphic Address :
  RECORDS TELEX, GLOUCESTER.

Any communications on the
subject of this letter should
be addressed to :

AIR OFFICER i/c RECORDS,

    Address as opposite,

and the following number
quoted :—

    Your Ref. : 07/1172570

RECORD OFFICE,

    ROYAL AIR FORCE,

        GLOUCESTER.

Date 13th September 1942

Dear Sir,

      I am glad to confirm that according to a
telegram from the International Red Cross Committee,
quoting Berlin information, your son No.1172570
Sergeant John Colin SEDGLEY of No.12 Squadron, Royal
Air Force, previously reported as 'missing' is now
a 'prisoner of war'. The report states he was
captured on 26th July 1942.

      Instructions for communicating with prisoners
of war are enclosed herewith.

             I am,
              Dear Sir,
              Your obedient Servant,

              Air Commodore,
              Air Officer i/c Records,
              ROYAL AIR FORCE.

H. Sedgley Esq.
47 Long Lane,
West Bromwich,
Staffordshire.

17th October 1942

Dear Dad, Mother and family

I was overjoyed to get your letters, I have received two from Rosa, one from Dad and one each from Arthur Jones and Harry Page. It is great to know that everyone is o.k. I hope Mother is better now, it was silly of her to worry about me. I am absolutely fine and feeling grand, so keep up the letter writing, all my love to you all and look after yourselves.

Cheerio for a bit, Col

The Arthur and Harry mentioned here were family friends and Rosa was his sister.

17th October 1942

Dear Dad, Mother and family

Happy as a king to know everyone is o.k. I am still feeling fine and waiting for plenty more letters. Tell anyone who can write to send a few lines, it does not matter who it is. Ask the lads at work to write, I'd love to hear from them. Tell Nadens that I am sorry but Johnny is dead. Could you send some chocolate soon? I will increase my allotment to you.

With all my love to everyone,

Col

The desire for contact with home is very clear in this letter; he was obviously becoming homesick. His request for chocolate gives some indication of the poor food the prisoners were receiving.

To his brother Harold

14th November 1942

Dear Harold,

How are things pal? I am in good health, good temper and extremely cheerful. I hope Myra is still o.k. Give her my love and tell her to do her stuff. I got mother's letter alright, I'm glad her arm is better. It is a pity I cannot be with you again this Xmas but there will be other Xmas's when things will be different.

Cheerio for a bit and all the best.

Col

Harold's wife, Myra, gave birth to a son (me) on 28th October 1942.

6th December 1942

Dear Dad, Mother and family

Well I am very glad to hear that everyone is o.k. at home. I am getting plenty of letters from you, I got one from Mother this morning dated 7th November 1942. I am feeling as well as ever so there is no need for you to worry about that. We have started to put up our Christmas decorations in the barrack and when we have finished it should look very nice. All I want now is Santa Claus to put something good in my stocking. I would like one of you to write to the Caterpillar Club care of Irving Parachute Co. Letchworth and ask them to send you a caterpillar. They issue them to all airmen whose lives have been saved by one of their parachutes. You will have to give them my rank service No. and squadron, and I wish you would thank them for me. I have not yet received any of your parcels but I expect to shortly. I want you to thank Nell for all the letters she has written. I will try to answer them sometime. I reckon that I should be an Uncle by now from what Harold told me, if so let me have a photo of the youngster as soon as possible, I'll see that we give him a good time on his first birthday. I shall be pleased to get a letter from Gwyn and Rita, I think all the kids ought to write sometime.

Ask Harry Hughes and Jack Edgley what they are waiting for will you? There is nothing for them to fear. I'll leave you now.

With all my love to everyone, Col

Many parcels sent from home never turned up and those that did had been opened and foodstuffs and anything else they thought useful removed by the Germans. Gwyn and Rita were Colin's younger brother and sister. Harry and Jack were friends.

13th December 1942

Dear Harold,

I can hardly tell you how pleased I was to hear that I am an Uncle, it was the best news I have had since I came here. I should love to be at home to see the little fellow and congratulate Myra and yourself personally, but I can wait. We shall have to bring him up to be an airman. I am still o.k. so do not worry about me. Hope all at home are alright. All the best old son, give my love to Myra and the baby and look after them.

Colin

I didn't become an airman; I became a metallurgist working in the heat treatment industry and later a Director of a heat treatment company based in West Bromwich.

20th December 1942
Dear Dad, Mother and family
Once again I am writing to let you know that I am going on alright, getting your letters and putting on weight. I weigh nearly ten stones now. Mother's letter comes regularly each week. I notice that her spelling is as good as ever. I was shocked to hear that Jean has started work again, I am worried about her getting a breakdown. Will you ask Harold to please write and give me three good reasons why he gave Fay her ring back. She can keep it for all I care, but I am engaged to no-one. I hope she realises that. Did Johnny get home to be godfather to the baby? I bet he'd be very proud of that job. He wrote a letter to me some time ago but he never finished it, he posted it with only half the first page written on, and never even signed it. It was nice to hear that Gran has got another house, it will make a great difference to her health, I hope we are in a different part of West Bromwich when I come home. I am starting school again shortly and I am taking industrial organisation and German, they will be useful after the war, there are quite a few little jobs I shall want to do when that day comes. Well that's all for now folks, so keep smiling.
With all my love to everyone
Col

Jean was his younger sister, who was of a nervous disposition. Colin had been engaged to Fay. Johnny was John Garland who was killed on 3rd December 1942. The baby was me. Colin was soon promoted to flight sergeant with effect from 1st February 1943.

13th February 1943
Dear Harold,
Received your letter of November today old son, glad to hear Myra and little Johnny are in the pink, I am fine as usual, I got 1100 cigarettes from home this week and I am in clover now. I am afraid Judy got his, so write to his home for me will you? Well I am waiting for the boat still, so keep that glass ready filled.

All the best kid, my love to Myra and Johnny.
Colin

Judy was a nickname for his friend John Garland, his surname being the same as the singer Judy Garland. The expression 'got his' refers to his being killed in action as previously described.

To his sister Nellie
6th June 1943
My dear Nell,
First of all I would like to thank you for all the letters you have written to me. If you stopped writing I hate to think of what I would do for correspondence. Well old girl, I am still quite well and I am not in chains now, I hope I never see another chain or piece of rope as long as I live, and I know I shall never forget last winter. We had a revue this week at the camp theatre, a few of the boys took the parts of girls and believe me I could not tell the difference. They were certainly some of the best looking girls I have seen for ages but unfortunately there were one or two differences. We also have here a military band, a dance band, a symphony orchestra and a theatre orchestra. All the players were more or less professionals in Civvy Street. Well my housekeeping is going along fine now, I can cook, on the occasions we have anything to cook, make beds, wash up, and wash clothes in cold water. There is only one housewife's duty that I cannot do. I shall make someone a good wife when I get home, any offers? All applications to be sent to me personally, I had Harold's letter in which he tells me about his nocturnal visitors, I thought at first that they had pinched Myra or the baby. That's all for now old kid, remember me to bill, the family and tell mother and dad not to worry, I'm quite o.k.
All my love, Colin

Colin mentions being chained, which started in October 1942 for the reasons previously explained. Winters in this part of Poland are particularly cold with temperatures down to minus 25 degrees centigrade. From his comments food is scarce and hot water non-existent for washing. I have no knowledge of my father's nocturnal visitors. Bill is Nellie's husband.

17th July 1943
Dear Dad, Mother and family,
I hope you are getting all my letters, I think I am getting most of yours. Well I am feeling absolutely fine these days and I am putting on weight faster than I thought possible. Yes we get all the medical attention we require here. We have our own medical officers and our own hospital. By the way we had a good

football match last Sunday night, Scotland who had the crack team here only managed to scrape a draw with Canada 3-3 and football is not the Canadians game. I have not heard louder cheering at the hawthorns, I hope you like the photograph. I am with a group of Birmingham boys. The chap standing on my left used to work at Accles, his name is Hadley. I wonder if Alex can pick me out? I bet he can. I have only had one clothing parcel since I came here, have you sent any more? The things I need most are razor blades, toothpaste, toothbrushes and socks. Incidentally, do not pay any more money for chocolate, you are flogging a dead horse. I have written to the 'Coach' they should have had my letter by now. I told Ike to keep a couple of barrels on one side as a reserve.

Let the lads at Smethwick see the photo won't you?

That's all for now so cheerio, all my love to you all

Colin

The Hawthorns is the home ground of West Bromwich Albion football team. Accles refers to Accles and Pollock, which was a tube making company based in Oldbury. The Coach he refers to is The Coach and Horses public house, local to the family home, with Ike being the licencee. Alex is his youngest brother.

Colin is third from right, standing.

7th August 1943
Dear Dad, Mother and family,
Your letters are still coming through o.k. I hope you are still getting mine regularly. Have you had my photo yet? I believe one of the lads has sent a photo to the evening despatch so keep your eyes open for it. It looks as though none of us need work again now glen has left school, what is she doing, labouring for a bricklayer? Incidentally, it's about time she wrote to me again. How did Rita get on in her scholarship exam? By the way when did you send the second clothing parcel? I have not had it yet and we have to rely on what is sent from home. Unless you do something about it soon I shall be wearing a grass skirt this winter. Well folks I am feeling very well lately, as you will see when you see my photograph and I have now taken up playing baseball. Naturally there is more shouting than action in it but we get some fun out of it. I was very amused to hear Mr. Atkins has gone in for the ice cream trade, I hope he makes a success of it. we had a big sports day here on august Monday the British Isle's versus the British Empire. We won rather easily. There was running, jumping, boxing, football and wrestling. It was a grand day, I wish Eric were here perhaps he could shake up Bruce a bit, I have not heard from him for weeks.

Well that's all for now all my love to everyone.
Colin

Glen is short for Glenis, one of his sisters. Rita was his youngest sister. I have no knowledge of Mr. Atkins, Eric or Bruce.

15th August 1943
Dear Dad, Mother and family,
Still feeling o.k. and getting your mail but no parcels for three months. I am certainly in need of another clothing parcel. I've only had one since I have been here. I've met some more West Bromwich soldiers Bert Hinton from Gladstone Street, Sam Cutler from Bayliss Street, Jim Hall from Wood Lane and a chap named Bowen from Sams Lane. Also a cousin of George Fisher's from Nechells and other chaps from Dudley and other local places.

Cheerio for a bit, all my love,
Colin

11th September 1943
Dear Dad, Mother and family,
Hope everyone is o.k. At home, I am feeling fitter and better than ever. I was not surprised to hear about Albert, I suppose he has taken to rum and a clay pipe now. He was just too fat to get among the monkeys and ice cream wasn't he? Those snaps you were going to send have been coming for twelve months now, what about it. Don't worry about me, I'm quite o.k.
All my love to you all
Col.

Albert is his younger brother, who had joined the Navy.

18th September 1943
Dear Dad, Mother and family
Its ages since I heard from you I hope everyone is o.k. at home. I shall probably get all your letters together shortly. This week I had my first parcel for months 200 Woodbines are you sure you sent them in the correct way? I should make sure if I were you. Well I am still going on fairly well, I've had a touch of flu this week but I am almost as good as new now in fact I am playing football tomorrow. I expect you thought that last letter was rather depressing didn't you? Well take no notice of it as we get that way sometimes it is only what we call an attack of barbed-wire blues. I have met a lot more chaps from Birmingham and district lately, we often spend hours arguing over the Albion, Villa and the Wolves etc. but as soon as we mention Drake to the Villa supporters they drop out. You'd be surprised how cheering it is to have lads from your own town around you. Well the sunbathing season is nearly over here now and we'll soon be putting on our winter furs again. I hope I do not have to spend many more winters here I never thought it could be so cold anywhere. Still as you say in your letters, it can't last forever. It can't not quite. How about all those snaps you where going to send last year? I'm still waiting.

That's all for now folks keep hoping,
All my love to you all
Colin

The Drake he is referring to here was footballer Ted Drake who, when playing for Arsenal during the 1930s, scored seven goals in a match against Aston Villa.

24th December 1943
Dear Dad, Mother and family,
I have just received letters from dad, Rosa and glen, a very nice Christmas box. I am feeling fine and looking forward to the New Year so that I can make a resolution not to send any more grumbling letters to you. We had our Red Cross Xmas parcels today and we are about to start on the feed we have been waiting for, so I will not be hungry over the festive season. I shall be thinking of you all and I hope that you have a good time. I may be with you some year.

All my love to you all.
Col.

Rosa and Glen were his younger sisters.

31st January 1944
Dear Harold,
Just to let you know I am still o.k., but I'm sorry to hear of little Johnny's illness, I hope he is quite well again now. I had another photo taken last week but I've found a better use for it this time. Football will be starting here again soon, I may have one or two games if I feel like it, to pass the time away. I had some cigs from the squadron last week again, I hope their funds don't fail or I will be in a state.

All the best pal, my love to Myra and John.
Colin

It was not until into my fifties that I became aware of that illness, mainly because my nephew Mark suffered with the same illness within the first year of his life. Mark was about six months old in hospital suffering with whooping cough, which can be quite serious. My family were discussing this when my mother said to my father, 'Remember when our John was a baby? He had that and when he started to recover he then had pneumonia, was given days to live by the doctor, but look at him now, a grown man.' Naturally I was stunned and asked the question, 'Why didn't you tell me earlier?' My mother replied, 'Well, did you really need to know?' On reflection I suppose I didn't. As for Colin, he was promoted to warrant officer on 1st February 1944.

14th August 1944
Dear Harold,

Just to let you know that I am keeping fine and hoping to be finer still soon, although they say that vodka is liable to affect one's stomach. I heard from Vic Hinton a short while ago. He's quite o.k. and like me, just dying to get his elbows propped up against the bar. How's Myra and Johnny? You promised to send me a photo of him, I wonder if that promise will ever materialise? Well old son I'll sign off, give my love to Myra, John and reserve that barrel,

All the best,
Col

With the prisoners knowing of the D-Day armies approaching from the west and the Russians from the east they were optimistic their incarceration would soon be over.

1st October 1944
Dear Harold,

How's things these days? o.k. I hope. I am pretty well and starting to settle down for my third winter here. I'm quite used to it, I'd hate to leave here now it would seem like leaving home. I suppose you have noticed I have been promoted to flight sergeant now, you'd all better have a few drinks to celebrate it. Hope Myra and John are keeping well I bet he will not know me when I come home.

Well that's all for now, chin up keep smiling, soon now,
Cheerio
Col

26th November 1944
Dear Harold,

I got your too much-censored letters of June and August this week, also photo of John, he's certainly a very bonny kid, I'm dying to see him. You said in your June letter "home for Xmas definite" well am I? I'm afraid I'm a member of a family of incurable optimists, I'll tell you something shall I? "Home for next Xmas maybe!" I'm keeping fairly well (rest of sentence censored) Well son, that's all for now my love to Myra and John keep smiling a little longer all the best
Col

December 1944 date unknown

Dear Dad, Mother and family

I have not heard from you for ages now but I am hoping to get a pile of letters some time soon. I hope everyone at home is keeping well and I trust by the time you get this you will have had a good Xmas. Personally I shall be very glad when it has gone although it is just the same as a ordinary day here. I'm afraid you had better stop sending parcels it's useless I never get any. The one you sent in march containing shirts and slippers I think we can safely write off as a dead loss, in any case they would not be a lot of use now you've no idea how cold it can get in this part of the world. If ever you do decide to send another clothing parcel try to get a good thick blanket and make up the rest with chocolate it will help a lot for next winter and please don't write back and say that I won't be here next winter because you've said that ever year and no one can tell. Well I will be twenty-five next month (11th January 1945) I think I'll have to save my bread ration for a week or so and give a party. By the way you will no doubt be pleased to hear of my promotion to warrant officer. I was flight sergeant on 1st May 1943 and w.o. on 1st February 1944. My present rank is now equivalent to the army rank of r.s.m. (regimental sergeant major).

Photograph taken at Stalag VIII-B/344. Colin is standing fifth from the right, the only one not wearing a tie. Others I have identified are: on the front row second from left, Arthur E. Adams; front row centre, Frank Firman; and on the front row far right, Ronald Arnold.

I bet I put Arch and Al through their paces when I get home. In my previous letter I mentioned I'd met a Hill Top lad who used to work for Pawsons named Bill Day. Well at present he is in dock having shrapnel taken from his chest but is doing very well. That's all for now so I'll say cheerio, don't forget bags of chocolate in future clothing parcels.

All my love to everyone,
Col

His promotion to flight sergeant was actually effective from 1st February 1943, though he was obviously not aware of this at the time. Arch and Al were his brothers Albert and Arthur. Pawsons was a clothes shop located at Carters Green, West Bromwich. Hill Top is also a part of the town.

The main theme of all of Colin's letters was to reassure his family that he was quite well; in fact he mentions in one letter that he is putting on weight but with the diet he and his fellow prisoners were on this couldn't be further from the truth.

The daily German rations were typically a cup of coffee made from barley or chicory, sometimes three small boiled potatoes with jackets on, a cup of soup made with turnips or swedes which sometimes included horsemeat. A loaf of black bread was shared between ten men and occasionally a pound of margarine shared by twenty men and lastly a cup of mint tea.

This starvation diet was augmented by Red Cross parcels, without which the prisoners would have starved to death.

These parcels usually contained a tin of meat such as spam, a tin of salmon, butter or margarine, cheese, sugar, dried milk, biscuits, soap, some had dried fruit and chocolate, and last but not least cigarettes.

The full contents of the parcels were not always given to the prisoners at the same time; they were given as single items on a daily basis. When tins were issued they were punctured by the Germans to prevent hoarding.

The prisoners lived in huts with approximately a hundred inmates; they slept in bunks with bed boards covered by a thin straw mattress. Some of the bed boards were used as fuel for the blower stoves the prisoners had constructed to heat water, food and give a little warmth in the winter. The huts were otherwise unheated.

Each hut had a commander elected by the residents of the hut with which the Germans communicated their orders.

There was no hot water and at times no cold water; if the prisoners were lucky they had a cold-water shower every six months. The toilet facility consisted of huts known by the prisoners as the 'forty seater' - each had to service approximately one thousand men. Queues were a normal occurrence.

The prisoners suffered from many diseases such as dysentery, typhus, typhoid, diphtheria, pneumonia and were covered in lice and fleas. The hospital, however, was one of the best at any camp - manned by doctors and orderlies who were prisoners themselves. Even with this care approximately 500 prisoners died from these diseases and other causes.

These conditions resulted in many of the prisoners being in a very poor physical condition with a low morale. By January 1945 they knew the Allies were fighting their way towards them from the west and the Russian army from the east and were hopeful that their ordeal would soon be over. But it was not to be; their greatest ordeal was yet to come.

The Lamsdorf Death March

As the Russian armies advancing west had now reached the Oder river, the prisoners at Stalag 344 could faintly hear gunfire and were naturally elated. On the night of 21st January 1945 the prisoners were told to prepare to move out the next morning; they were given a complete Red Cross parcel and a blanket, collected their few other possessions and the following morning, in groups of two to three hundred, they were marched under guard towards the north-west.

The winter that year was one of the coldest for some time, with snow several feet deep with night temperatures of minus 25 degrees centigrade. Physically the men were in a weak condition having endured years of poor rations, with their clothes not being suitable for the appalling weather. Nevertheless, they were marched 20 to 30 kilometres a day through blizzards across country, resting at night in barns, factories, churches and even in the open. When the Red Cross parcels had been depleted there was little food available. The men resorted to scavenging to survive; they ate dogs, cats, rats even grass.

As they passed through the countryside and villages some of the German inhabitants gave them what food they could - others wished to hang them, especially aircrew in retaliation for the now almost constant bombing by the RAF and US air force. At such times the marching aircrew hid their uniforms by covering themselves with their blankets. They marched on with the occasional rest day, their physical condition deteriorating daily, with many being frozen to death or succumbing to disease.

Colin did not talk to me much about this march other than saying that most of the men went through periods when they were exhausted and felt they could not walk another step, and their comrades stepped in and helped or dragged them along until they recovered somewhat and they in their turn could help the next man in distress. He related that when he sat one night huddled together with his fellow prisoners for warmth in a barn, with the outside temperature well below freezing and a blizzard blowing, he made a vow that if he survived this ordeal and got home he would get roaring drunk on his next birthday, 11th January 1946.

The prisoners marched on throughout February and marched on a route that passed close to Dresden. The weather, even in the middle of March, was still awful with temperatures below freezing. Some time during late March or early April 1945, still on a north-west course, they passed north of Hanover and south-west of the town of Bergen and saw something that they would never forget. They marched past the Belsen extermination camp; the smell was indescribable and the sight of people moving about with skeletal bodies was horrific.

Liberation

The prisoners were finally marched to Stalag XI-B at Fallingbostel, Lower Saxony, arriving at an overcrowded camp with prisoners of all services and nationalities, including American prisoners from the Battle of the Bulge. The camp was in a deplorable state, with lack of food and medicines. The prisoners from Stalag 344 had marched approximately 1000 kilometres. Colin was covered in boils, suffering from acute exhaustion and malnutrition but thankfully alive. I recall him saying to me 'We take some killing', meaning I believe, we being our family. (This reminds me of my flirt with death during my first year of life.) Gunfire could now be heard most of the time with aircraft passing overhead regularly. With no clear front line and heavy fighting all around, the prison camp was actually the safest place to be.

On 6th April 1945 the Germans marched out those prisoners that could march north away from the advancing Allied army. Left behind were about 5,000 men who were suffering from illness or the effects of the march. Colin was one of those. On the morning of 16th April 1945, Colin and the rest of the prisoners at Stalag XI-B were liberated by the British 7th

Armoured Division. The tanks that liberated the camp were members of the 8th Kings Royal Irish Hussars.

On this day the Russians launched the final major offensive of the European theatre of war, their objective to take Berlin. This battle alone, which lasted until 2nd May, when the German garrison finally surrendered, was at a cost of over 80,000 Russian and Polish troops dead and missing, and 280,000 wounded.

Home to England

Colin and many of his fellow prisoners were very poorly and were repatriated as soon as aircraft were available. He arrived back in England and was sent to 106 Personnel reception centre, at RAF Cosford in Shropshire, and then into the hospital next door. His first letter home from there is now very fragile.

23rd April 1945
Dear Dad, Ma and kids
Well this is just about the most wonderful thing imaginable isn't it. It still seems like a dream to me, I'll tell you what happened. At 08.40 on the morning of April 16th (Monday) Monty's merry men in the form of the 7th Armoured Division appeared outside the wire of Stalag XI-B at Fallingbostel and boy! what a reception they got, one of the lads got out of the tank, walked up to the wire and shouted 'Any English boys here?' We soon let him know and then he started lobbing over Woodbines and the first white bread we'd seen since we left Blighty.

I'm in dock now with a perforated eardrum but in a few days I hope to be out and at home. You may be able to visit me if I'm here this weekend. I'll make enquires, I'll ring dad up some time this week so he'd better keep his ears open. Now don't worry about me and don't get impatient, I'll soon be with you. Cheerio for a little while folks, and remember no panic or fuss when I get home, keep everything quiet.

All my love to you all, Col
p.s. I'm afraid its got to be Shandies for me for quite a time so cancel the barrel.

Colin did not mention his real condition, that he weighed just 112 pounds, or that he would need some time to recover from his ordeal.

Victory in Europe finally came on 8th May 1945, marking the formal acceptance by the Allied forces of Nazi Germany's unconditional surrender of it's armed forces.

Colin was discharged from hospital on 14th May and returned home to Lyng Lane. While he was recovering physically, how he was recovering mentally, having experienced the hardships he had endured, I do not know - but knowing him in later in life I think he put it all behind him. However, I believe to his dying day he never forgot his closest friends who sadly lost their lives, John Naden and John Garland.

Colin in July 1945, well on his way to recovery.

During this summer, at a dance in Wolverhampton, Colin met his future wife Dorothy May Lewis - Aunt Dot to me. They were married on 15th December 1945 at St. Marks Church in Chapel Ash, Wolverhampton. (This church was decommissioned in 1978, and a new church built - as a listed building, the original church being converted for office use, retaining its exterior.) Colin's elder brother Harold, my father, was the best man.

The happy couple.

LESLIE L. IRVIN
F.R.Ae.S., F.R.S.A.
HONORARY SEC.
EUROPEAN BRANCH

c/o IRVING AIR CHUTE
OF GREAT BRITAIN LTD.
ICKNIELD WAY
LETCHWORTH, ENGLAND

CATERPILLAR CLUB

November 23, 1945.

W/O. J. C. Sedgley,
c/o. 47, Lyng Lane,
WEST BROMWICH.
Staffs.

Dear W/O. Sedgley,

On receipt of your letter of November 9th, I ordered your Caterpillar Pin, and requested our suppliers to hurry it through so that you could have it for your wedding.

I am pleased to say that it has just been received, and I have pleasure in sending it to you herewith, with our compliments and the hope that it brings you Good Luck.

Wishing you both every happiness, I am,

Yours sincerely,

Sec. to L. Irvin.

MEL.
Encl. Pin.

The Caterpillar Club was started in 1922 by the Irvin Chute Company, awarding a tiny gold Caterpillar Pin to anyone who saved his life by parachuting from a disabled or flaming aircraft.

Prior to this, on 4th October, Colin's rank was reclassified as warrant officer (aircraftman second class, wireless operator 2). On 13th November, he was posted to an aircraft maintenance unit; his service record does not give the number of the unit in question. At that time there were some one hundred 100 of these types of units across the country, so I do not know the actual location of his posting - however, I have a feeling it would have been close to home and therefore could have been Lichfield or Cosford.

It was in May 1946 that I believe Colin finally asked to be released from service, his reason being he had skills that would be valuable in civilian life. The majority of releases were Class A, according to age and length of service. His release class was B., the B. indicating his request was in relation to skills useful in post-war reconstruction. The request was accepted and he was released from service on 1st June at No. 100 personnel despatch centre, located at Uxbridge, Middlesex. His life as a member of the RAF was over, his life as a husband and father was beginning.

Back in Civvy Street

After their marriage Colin and Dorothy lived with Colin's sister Nell and her husband Bill in Thomas Street, West Bromwich. Their only child Linda (pictured overleaf) was born there on 13th February 1947.

Colin resumed work at Accles and Pollock in Oldbury for a while, but decided to try the pub trade and became a licencee. He managed a pub owned by Mitchells and Butlers in Tantany Lane for approximately two years. It was called The Windmill. He then returned to Midland Motor Cylinder Company, Smethwick, working in the production control department - where he stayed until his retirement, attaining the position of senior production manager.

Within a few years, Colin, Dorothy and Linda were happily living in their own house at 221 Hampstead Road, Great Barr, Birmingham. The years passed with Colin putting all his war experiences to the back of his mind. In the course of time Linda married Philip Wood, who was serving in the Royal Navy and they had two children, Ian and Sarah. Colin and Dorothy, like most grand parents, doted on the children and were enjoying their lives.

It was not until 1981 that an event happened which was to bring Colin's memories of the war flooding back.

The town council of Nijkerk decided to commemorate local people who were part of the wartime resistance against Nazi Germany by naming a

Left: Colin and Dorothy in 1967.
Right: Their daughter, Linda.

The Windmill Inn, 18 Tantany Lane, West Bromwich, courtesy of Terry Price.

street (Resistance Avenue) after them. Henk Sietsma, one of the resistance leaders, set out to trace a certain RAF airman who had been betrayed by a traitor in their midst, not knowing if he had even survived the war.

Colin was that airman, who was soon to return to Holland after 39 years. Colin decided to write of the events leading to this return visit and his thoughts and impressions. These are reproduced as he wrote them at that time.

Invitation and Re-union - in Colin's own words

It all happened when the former mayor of West Bromwich, Councillor Eric Owen, caused to be printed in the 'Evening Mail' of 23rd May 1981 (Saturday), an appeal by a Mr. Henk Siestsma of Pijlakker, Holland, for information concerning the whereabouts of former RAF sergeant t.c. Sedgley, whom he had met for the first time on the morning of Sunday 26th July 1942, at a farm near Nijkerk, in the vicinity of Amersfoort. Mr. Sietsma wrote of some of the activity of that day and of the efforts which were made by him and the farmer's family to prevent the airman's capture by the occupying German forces. He also detailed the type of aircraft (Vickers Wellington), the aircraft No., the target for the raid on the night of the 25th July (Duisburg), the squadron No. (no. 12), also the fact that one of the member of the crew (John Naden) had been killed in the very early hours of that Sunday.

I did not personally see this newspaper article and it was brought to my attention by my brother Albert who had been told of it by Gwyn, our younger brother.

On Monday morning 25th May 1981, I telephoned Councillor Owen at his home in Tipton and he kindly invited me to visit him to read the actual letter, I went to his house that same morning, obtained a copy of the letter and had a long conversation with the councillor and his wife. At the same time we enjoyed quite a few glasses of his excellent home-brewed ale.

The following day, I wrote to Mr. Sietsma and said that because of the accurate details he had given, I had no doubt that we had met 39 years ago although I did not recall his name. This, of course, was a foolish comment to make because obviously under the circumstances prevailing at that time the last thing he would do would be to reveal his identity. The one certain thing, however, is that I distinctly remembered the farmer, his wife and his son. These were the people with whom I had made my first contact after parachuting into Holland.

One week later I received a telephone call from Henk Sietsma informing me that he was coming to England on Monday 22nd June and that he would be at our home at about midday. A letter confirming this arrived the following day. I advised Councillor Owen of this and he consulted the present Mayor, Councillor Sid Pemberton who arranged a formal reception at 1.00 pm in the Mayor's Parlour at West Bromwich town hall.

At 12.15 pm on the appointed day (22nd June 1981) Henk arrived and after greeting each other continental fashion I introduced him to my wife Dorothy. I could still not positively recognise him but he was absolutely certain that I am the man he helped so long ago. It must be said that Henk spent the last 18 months of the war in Dachau concentration camp; so one could hardly expect to identify him as the young man of 21 years of age.

From left to right: Mayor Sid Pemberton, Colin, Henk Sietsma, Dorothy, Mrs. Owen, Eric Owen, the Mayoress Mrs Pemberton.

He brought us presents of a Dutch teapot stand, two candles and a set of pretty blue Dutch table napkins, with which Dorothy was delighted. At 12.45 pm the mayoral car arrived and we drove to the town hall to be received by the mayor, the Mayoress and Councillor Owen and Mrs Owen. After drinks and a lot of conversation, we had lunch in the Gala

Baths restaurant, and then returned to the parlour where local pressmen were waiting to take statements and photographs. These appeared in the 'Sandwell Mail' and the 'Evening Mail' on the following day (23rd June) true to their record of consistent inaccuracies, my age was given as 71!! Still an error of only 10 years cannot be too bad.

However Henk had to be in London by 6.00 pm, so the whole company again in the Mayor's car escorted him to New Street station where we saw him on to his train at 3.30 pm before leaving he again insisted that Dorothy and I go to Holland for official receptions and celebrations of our first meeting.

We gave a firm promise to be there and this we did, although, due to various circumstances, we were unable to be in Holland on Monday 27th July 1981, the date that the Dutch would have preferred.

The visit - Friday 24th July 1981

Our party of four set out by national coach from Digbeth coach station, Birmingham, to travel to London, Dover, Calais and then to Amsterdam. The party consisted of Dorothy, myself, my brother Albert and his wife Theresa.

We left Digbeth at 08.45, carrying seven other passengers, these having already travelled from Manchester and we reached Victoria coach station at 12.00 midday. The journey through the London suburbs had been very slow due to the preparations for the royal wedding on 29th July (Prince Charles and Diana Spencer).

The coach filled up with passengers in Victoria and we did the next stage of the trip in good time, arriving in Dover at a little after 2.00 pm after passing through passport control we went into the duty-free shop, bought our whiskey, cigarettes etc, and boarded the hovercrafts. Thirty minutes later we were in Calais. At about 4.30 pm the coach began its journey through France, Belgium and Holland, mainly on the motorways. We stopped once, in Belgium, for a meal etc. and by this time everyone was feeling rather travel weary and looking forward to the end of the day. It came, for us when we arrived at the Interland hotel, Amsterdam at 11.00 pm. The proprietor of the hotel showed us our rooms and told me that a Mr. Sietsma had telephoned a short time previously and wished me to ring him as soon as possible. I rang him and we had a brief conversation relative to the itinerary for the next day and then Al, Theresa, Dorothy and I sat in our room and had a nightcap, eventually getting into bed at about

12.45 am. We had by then, agreed that in future all of our long distance travel would be by air.

Saturday 25th July 1981

Breakfast comprised of ham, cheese, boiled eggs, bread, butter, jam and marmalade with as much tea or coffee as we wished. After this we went to our rooms to await the arrival of Henk and Jani (his wife) the time was then 08.30 hours. At 09.00 hours we walked into the small foyer to find that they had just appeared. We had not previously met Jani so after introductions we had a brief conversation, mainly about the weather, which was threatening to spoil our day. Jani like Henk, speaks excellent English and is a charming and vivacious person. At 09.45 hours we said a temporary "cheerio" to Al and Theresa and got into Henk's car to begin what proved to be a most emotional though exhausting day. It was also a day of great joy.

We drove out of Amsterdam and, after a little more than an hour, we were well into the farming areas and approaching the town of Nijkerk where, 39 years minus one day ago, I had paid a brief visit, arriving on that occasion by parachute, we were shown by Henk the place where the wellington crashed into the ground, also the spot were the four surviving aircrew members came to earth. All of this however was from a distance of several miles. On the outskirts of Nijkerk we stopped to look at the school where Henk's father had been headmaster and where Henk spent

The Niebeek farm buildings.

his boyhood. Then it was time for the great event of the day, my reunion with the farmer and his family.

Shortly after 11.00 hours we turned off a narrow road and drove into the farmyard where I had made my first contact after my unplanned visit of so many years ago. A door opened and out stepped Brand Niebeek. His first words, in Dutch, were "Colin when we first met, you had light brown wavy hair, your face, however, has not changed much in 39 years." (Perhaps I looked 61 years old when I was 22).

Then came the moment I had been awaiting. My very own Dutch farmer, Albert Niebeek, appeared in the doorway and I stepped forward to greet him. As we shook hands and looked closely at each other, the intervening years slipped away and I was then 100% certain that I was again facing the brave man who had risked his live and the lives of his family to help me. He turned to Henk and said, "It is him alright, I have no doubts at all." This, to me, was one of the most touching moments of my life and it was only with great difficulty that I kept back the tears. This grand old man of nearly 89 years of age had remembered me almost immediately and I was told later that the events of Sunday 26th July 1942 were related regularly by him to his children and grandchildren over the years. So much so that they were able to fill me in on some details.

Dorothy had by now met Brand and his father and exchanged greetings with them through Henk and Jani who, throughout the whole day, acted

Opa, Colin and Brand in the farmhouse.

as interpreters. We were then taken inside the farmhouse where we met brand's wife Wolltje (pronounced *volchee*) and their sons and daughters. Other relatives and friends were also present. In the dining room coffee and biscuits were served and we sat around a large table reminiscing, again though Henk and Jani, on the events of nearly 40 years ago. It should be pointed out here that many details have been forgotten or even distorted in the passage of time and on occasions we found ourselves virtually prompting each other. Nevertheless, we who had been involved in the events of 1942 knew without any shadow of doubt that we had met in this place long ago and under quite different circumstances.

In the meantime Dorothy did a wonderful job of communication with the ladies and children of the family, irrespective of the language problem. How do women do this? It seems to me that all women, no matter what their nationality and tongue may be, speak the same language. Most men will agree with this theory and must therefore also agree that we men could learn something from this fact.

The pleasure and happiness of our joyful re-union was then rudely shattered by a minor invasion. The press arrived!! This was something I personally had not expected or desired, being by nature a rather shy person and reluctant to be the subject of publicity. There was however nowhere to run so we all settled down to the interviews, or should I say interrogations?

Dorothy and I were asked to give our thoughts and feelings on our meeting with the Niebeeks and the Sietsmas. Of course we had to say, very truthfully, that this was a fantastically happy day for us, a dream-like day which we can never forget. I also told the reporters that it was my fervent hope that this is only the beginning of a long and deep friendship with these fine Dutch people.

Henk, Brand and I were asked many questions about our first meeting and the action which was taken to help me to evade the Germans and I was also requested to give some detail of my eventual capture and how I spent the rest of the war. One unexpected question put to me was "Did I know the identity of the man who betrayed me and probably other RAF men?" I did not know this man's identity and despite pressing the reporter for an answer, I was not told until after we had returned home. In any case it does not really matter now but at least I have a name. I had often wondered about this. Now I can forget it.

The newsmen and their photographers, after many pictures inside the farmhouse, then ushered us outside into the cold rain and took more photographs in the relevant areas of the farmyard. This took approximately half an hour and we were all grateful to go back inside where the busy Wolltje had lunch ready for us. We sat down, Henk said grace, and we all enjoyed a very appetising meal.

After lunch a little convey of cars left the farm for our engagement in the town of Nijkerk. Dorothy and I travelled with Henk and Jani in their car, preceded by Brand, Wolltje and Opa and followed by two ex-resistance men, Henk Van Veluw and Jan Meerveld and their wives. The last car contained reporters, Paul and Schneider, plus one other newsman whose name we cannot recall. It took us nearly half an hour to arrive at the outskirts of Nijkerk and there seemed to be a lot activity ahead of us. As we drove into the small town it was Dorothy who said, "Surely this is not for us!" Union Jacks were flying beside the Dutch flags and one large Union Jack was flying at the top of the town hall. People in the streets were smiling and waving to us and I shrank back into my seat trying to become invisible. The cars stopped a few yards from the main town hall entrance and we all alighted. Then as we began to walk towards the steps a carillon of 47 bells in the tower of Nijkerk church pealed out the English national anthem. I felt proud, humble and embarrassed at one and the same time. It was yet another touching moment in a very touching day.

We entered the town hall and were received by the burgomeester, his wife and members of the council, all in full regalia. Behind them came surviving members of the wartime Dutch resistance and local dignitaries and businessmen followed these. After many introductions our party was escorted upstairs to the council chamber where, after cigarettes, cigars and a glass of fine gin, the Mayor addressed the gathering in both English and Dutch.

He spoke of the appalling conditions in Holland during the Nazi occupation and of how people at night lay in their beds awaiting the sound of R.A.F. Bombers approaching from the west, passing overhead, then vanishing into the east in the direction of Germany. Many people he said would then remain awake until, in the early morning they heard the same aircraft returning on their way back to England. This gave the Dutch people their main hope of eventual liberation and gave them the inspiration and courage to fight a continual underground war against the Nazis also to help any Allied airman who suddenly found himself alone in hostile territory. History shows that they did precisely this. It was then the turn of Henk Sietsma to speak and he related in some detail the events of the 26th July 1942. He told the assembled company of my arrival at the Niebeek's farm early on that Sunday morning and of the immediate and unconditional willingness of Mr. Albert Niebeek (Opa) and his son Brand to give me all possible assistance whilst knowing full well that the penalty for helping an RAF man was almost certain death. Executions had been carried out in a nearby district a few weeks previously for this very offence. Henk then went on to tell of his arrival, later that morning, at the farm and of the civilian clothing he brought with him. He told of our journey to the nearby woods and the arrangement to collect me at midnight when he would whistle our national anthem. Unfortunately for me it was a squad of heavily armed Germans who entered the woods at about 7.00 pm and came directly to where I was hiding.

At this state in his speech I hoped that he would name the informer but for some reason he did not. He did however speak of the fact that although I was interrogated by the Germans intensively and at great length, not one German ever went to the farm to question the Niebeeks. In a short reply to Henk, Brand said "We only did what we had to do" and to me this seemed to be the most modest statement I had ever heard.

Henk Van Veluw, whom I have previously mentioned, then stood up and made a brief speech, in Dutch, and approached our table. We again shook hands and he presented me with a set (2) of parachute harness clips. The burgomaster informed me that Mr. Van Vuluw had retrieved these from the body of John Naden, the crew member who had died in a field on that July morning in 1942. He had gone out when he heard the noise of the crashing Wellington and had a thorough search. It is apparent that on this occasion at least, the Dutch were one move ahead of the Germans.

Then Henk Van Veluw left our table. The burgomaster's wife, presented Dorothy with a large and beautiful bouquet of locally grown flowers and other ladies in the company did the same so that in a very few minutes we were literally buried in blooms. Dinie Meerveld also gave to Dorothy a small plaque of Nijkeek church and this we thought was a wonderful gesture from a very brave little women because for three and a half years of the war she had hidden in her house a family of 3 Jews (father, mother and daughter) and this in Nazi-occupied Europe was probably the gravest offence of all. These then were the people who were bestowing honours upon us!!!

After a further brief speech, the burgomaster came to me, followed by an usher, who unwrapped a brown paper parcel. Inside was a magnificent

Henk Van Veluw presenting John Naden's parachute clips to Colin.

engraving of old Nijkerk. This work had been specially commissioned and was given to us on behalf of all the townspeople of Nijkerk in thanks for the contribution, which they say I made, to eventual victory in the Netherlands. I stood up to speak but words were difficult to find and even when I found them I found it practically impossible to utter them. So, after a few phrases in which I thanked everyone present, I sat down feeling very small and extremely churlish. I have since written to the burgomaster and thanked him and all concerned in a proper manner.

A further surprise was in store for us before we left the town hall. Mrs Maartje Van Veluw showed to us some old photographs. They were of the curtains in her house and these were made from my parachute which her husband had eventually found hidden in the side of a dyke on his land where I had buried it. It is not everyone who has silk curtains and I would nominate Henk Van Veluw as the Dutch champion parachute hunter!

It was now time to go so we all walked about 100 yards to Nijkerk church where we were welcomed by the verger an English-speaking young man bearing the name of Hank. He related to us at great length, the history of this fine building, which at one time consisted in fact of 2 wooden buildings, originally constructed about 500 years ago for worship in the Roman Catholic faith. It would appear that, due to constant flooding in this low-lying area of Holland, the wooden buildings were eventually demolished and the present brick-built church was constructed on higher ground. It is now - and has been for many years - a protestant church.

At a little after 5.00 pm we left the church. We thanked the verger for his excellent and interesting lecture and on the forecourt we expressed our gratitude to the burgomaster, the councillors and everyone else and said our goodbyes. We were given assurances that we would be welcomed in Nijkerk at any time and we do intend to go there again. Our 3 cars drove out of the town in the direction of the Zuiderzee. In the first car were the Van Veluws and the Meervelds, in the second were Brand, Wolltje and Opa and in the last Henk, Jani, Dorothy and myself. It was still very dull and the rain was drizzling down although there were signs that the clouds were beginning to break up. As we drove along, Henk pointed out many places of interest, particularly the work constantly being carried out on reclamation of the land from the sea. However, the poor weather and the appearance of sea mists restricted visibility to a great extent but we have promised ourselves a longer visit in the future so that we can spend more time in this desolate but fascinating part of Holland. After about half an hour the leading car stopped in an isolated area and we got out and looked at the spot where my aircraft had crashed.

Obviously there is now no indication of this but it was a strange experience to stand a few yards from the spot and look and think. A little wetter we got back into the cars and drove on for 15 minutes and again got out to look across the polder (field) on our right, to the place where the other four in the crew landed. One, as we know, died on this spot and the other three unknowingly walked towards a nearby German army camp and were promptly captured. Then, two miles further on and on our left, we came to the place where I first touched the soil of Holland. To reach it we had to leave the road and walk nearly half a mile along the top of the dyke itself. The actual landing spot was about 50 yards into the polder from the broad ditch and I remembered very well digging furiously with my hands into the earth on the side of the dyke, just above the water level, in order that I could put the parachute, at least for a time, our of sight. In the prevailing weather conditions it would have been inadvisable to follow on foot the route I took in 1942, so Brand pointed out the direction in which I had gone and it was quite easy to see the narrow dirt roads over the dykes which did and still do, lead to the Niebeek's farm. Memories came back to me of that journey, sometimes running, sometimes walking in that very early summer morning! I thought at that time that I must have been

The spot where the Wellington crashed.

Brand indicating to the wood in the far distance, now less than a third of its original size. Note he is wearing Dutch clogs.

Henk, Kurt (Brand's son), Brand, Colin and Opa discussing were Colin slept on that morning of Sunday 26th July 1942.

moving for several hours but in fact it was a little over an hour before I first asked Albert Niebeek "Can you help me?"

We now had to say goodbye to our friends the Van Veluws and the Meervelds and this we did with promises that we would all meet again at the earliest possible opportunity, then we returned to the farm.

After several cups of hot tea, Brand, Henk and I put on rubber boots and walked out across the fields. We passed through Brand's herd of cattle and came to a deep, wide ditch, forded by a plank of wood roughly 12 feet long, 10 inches wide and 2 inches thick. The top surface was caked with slippery mud and slime and looked positively lethal. Henk and I surveyed it with some trepidation, or could it have been sheer terror.

However the brave and gallant Brand assured us that there was nothing to fear and volunteered to make the initial crossing. We stood back and told him to go ahead. He very gingerly placed one foot onto the board and with a nervous grin, placed his other foot in front of the first. Then he rashly transferred his weight to the front foot, whereupon his rubber boot immediately skidded violently from the board, the board turned completely over, revealing it's bottom surface and Brand was projected at great speed through the air and splashed down, base over apex (or words to that effect), into nearly five feet of very cold water.

He quickly surfaced and scrambled up the side muttering furiously in his native language. I have no idea what he said. Henk and I then had to turn our backs on Brand because we had seen something very interesting in the direction of the farmhouse, which was still just visible. We did really try though unsuccessfully, to make sympathetic noises. Henk was the next to cross and he did this while Brand on the other side gripped his end of the board in both hands and I did the same on my side, still trying desperately to look serious. Then whist the two of them held the board on their side I quickly nipped across, arms out stretched, looking and feeling like the sugar plum fairy.

On this side of the ditch now was what remains of the wooded area in which I had hidden during the afternoon and evening of the 26th July 1942. It was not possible to pinpoint the exact spot because over the years most of the trees had been felled and it was only a preservation order by the Dutch government a few years ago, which saved this wood from disappearing altogether. It has now dwindled to less than a third of its original size, I was told, but had already noticed, that wooded areas are quite rare in Holland.

We then retraced our steps towards the farm, negotiated the ditch without further mishap and arrived in the house to find most of the family preparing to go out to dinner. The exceptions were Brand's sons Bert, Ab

Viewing the area where Colin landed in July 1942.

and Kurt who had to remain to milk the cows and generally attend to farm matters.

The dinner had been arranged at a restaurant in Spakenburg, a small town situated along a most attractive harbour and approximately ten miles from the farm. We travelled in 2 cars, Opa, Brand and Wolltje in the first and Henk, Jani, Dorothy and myself following. On our arrival we were welcomed by the headwaiter and shown to our table where we drank an aperitif and ordered our meals. Dorothy and I ordered soup followed by veal but we do not recall the choice of the others. Everything was beautifully cooked and served and whilst we were enjoying it a lively conversation was carried on, again with the help of Henk and Jani. It was plain to see that Opa was having one of the happiest days of his life! So were we all.

Midway through the main course, the proprietor approached our table and, after saying that he recognised us from the photographs and written reports on the front pages of the local evening newspapers, he informed us that the head chef had prepared a special sweet in honour of the guests from England. This of course, came as a complete surprise to us and for a few moments we just did not know what to say but eventually we expressed our warmest thanks to him and all members of his staff for this most friendly and generous gesture. Being anything but an expert on food I can only describe this last course as a crème-caramel surrounded by fresh

Spakenburg in the province of Ultrecht. Photograph by Michielverbeek (CC BY-SA 3.0.).

strawberries and cream. Also Union Jacks were very much in evidence around the serving dishes.

After again thanking the proprietor, headwaiter and the other staff for their wonderful service and promising to visit them again at some future date, we left the restaurant and at Jani's suggestion, went for a short after-dinner walk along the harbour. The rain had temporarily ceased and the sun had broken through the clouds, turning the water and the moored boats into a picturesque, multi-hued canvas of brilliant colour. It all looked as though everything, the sea, the small houses, the harbour wall and even the people, many in traditional Dutch dress, had been freshly painted a few minutes earlier. It was a scene, which I will personally never forget. Wolltje and Dorothy walked arm in arm, Jani and I linked arms on either side of Opa and Henk and Brand strolled along behind. Everyone was talking though we all spoke the same language and again I felt that we do!

The fresh invigorating air was very welcome after the hours we had spent indoors or in a car throughout the day, but time goes on and at 9.00 pm we knew that we had to leave the beautiful little town of Spakenburg.

To return to Amsterdam we had to travel in the opposite direction to the route the Niebeeks would have to take to their farm so we said goodbye to them on the car park. They left no doubt in our minds that this was only the beginning of the renewal of the friendship which had begun 39 years previously. Dorothy and I assured them that we would never lose contact with them again and this is one thing upon which we were determined. Our feelings as they drove away were of happiness that we had spent some time in the company of these fine people and sadness that we had to leave them so soon. Jani decided to drive this time so Dorothy sat with her in the front passenger seat and Henk and I occupied the rear seats, trying to get comfortable without damaging the many bouquets of flowers which had been given to us. We approached Amsterdam from a different direction and Henk again pointed out to us many places of interest that we had not previously seen. At 10.40 pm we arrived at the Interland hotel and our two great friends helped us to unload the gifts and mementoes we had received. Due to the late hour and the fact that they still had over an hours drive to their home in Pijnacker, they did not come into the hotel with us so once again we had to take our leave of someone whom we would have wished to remain with us for very much longer.

After such a day, full of ceremony, emotion, wonder and delight, it may be understood that we were both mentally and physically shattered although very, very happy. However after depositing all that we were carrying onto the beds, Dorothy went to the room occupied by Albert and Theresa, to let them know that we had returned. They immediately came down to our room with Al (bless him) carrying a bottle of scotch, or at least more than half a bottle. So, after filling the glasses, we told them of the events of the day and they, in turn gave us the story of their day which had been spent in Amsterdam sightseeing, shopping, eating and sampling the local brew, we were very pleased that they had had an enjoyable time. Then at 12.45 am we went to bed confident in the belief that we would sleep for 24 hours. In fact, my mind was still so over-active that I hardly slept at all.

Albert and Theresa.

Sunday 26th July 1981

At 8.30 am we sat down to another enormous Dutch breakfast and discussed our plans for the day. The rain had returned and the low, black clouds made us think more of January than July. However, Al and Theresa having found the previous day found several places in Amsterdam worthy of another visit, it was agreed that the four of us would spend the day in that charming city and see as much as we could. Before we could leave the hotel, I was "ambushed" by the proprietor Martin Van Der Zalm and taken into his private room to examine his prize possession, which turned out to be a very comprehensive history of Bomber Command activities over Germany, 1939 to 1945. Mr. Van Der Zalm said that he was very proud to have had us in his hotel and would be delighted if we would visit him again. We possibly will.

At 9.40 am we walked out into the rain and began a leisurely stroll around Amsterdam, taking in the museums, public buildings and quite a few sex shops, feeling in need of a little liquid refreshment at about mid-day, we went into a restaurant and ordered coffee for the ladies and beer for the gentlemen. After about an hour, Dorothy and Theresa suggested that we stay there for lunch so we enjoyed an excellent chicken meal, finished by coffee and brandy. The cost of this was amazingly low in comparison with UK prices.

We left the restaurant at 2.15 pm and walked rather aimlessly along many streets and over many canal bridges, then sat on a bench alongside a canal and watched the world go by. The rain had stopped at about 1.00 pm. Still feeling a little weary from our travels of the past 2 days, we decided to go back to our hotel and rest for an hour or so but before that we decided that we would like to see Anne Frank's house, so we consulted our street map and set off in the direction indicated. After more than an hour we saw no sign of the house so we tried to re-trace our footsteps of that morning but soon decided that we were lost. Theresa then bravely approached a policeman and asked for directions to the Interland hotel. The policeman, with a pitying look, pointed across the square and 3 minutes later we were in our rooms. We opened a bottle of gin which Dorothy had bought during that afternoon and at about 6.00 pm we lay down, hoping to sleep for an hour. This did not happen so we had a bath, put on some different clothes and went up to Albert and Theresa's room to find that they also were ready to go out again. So at 8.00 pm we were again on our travels and after walking through an area of Amsterdam which we had not previously seen, we went into a cosy little restaurant, had a drink and a light meal, and then returned to our hotel. I ordered very early breakfast for the next morning and, after half an hour discussing the events of the day, we went to bed at approximately 11.30 pm and slept soundly all night.

Monday 27th July 1981

I had set our travelling clock alarm for 5.45 am and by 6.00 am I had made a pot of tea, using our own immersion water heater, and at 7.00 am the four of us were in the dining room and prepared for our journey home. (Dorothy and Theresa had packed our cases the previous night). At 7.25 am the doorbell rang, as expected. It was the coach driver, who had promised to call for us at 7.30 so we carried the luggage plus the bouquets of flowers to the corner of the street, saw everything safely into the luggage compartment and took our seats. At 7.35 am we left to pick up other passengers from their various hotels and by 8.30 am we were on the outskirts of Amsterdam, travelling in the direction of the Belgium border.

Like us, most of our fellow passengers were rather tired and the journey to Calais was quite uneventful. We stopped once for coffee etc. At a restaurant in Belgium and arrived at our port of embarkation at 12.30 pm after passing through customs and passport control we left Calais, by hovercraft, at 2.00pm and arrived in Dover at 2.35 pm. again we queued, passports and duty free goods at the ready, and re-alighted onto our coach at a little after 3.00pm for the next stage of the journey, to London. The coach moved rather slowly particularly through the southern suburbs of London and we did not reach Victoria coach station until 5.40 pm and there we had to have a change of driver. The new driver arrived promptly at 5.45 pm and informed us that he would have to take the coach away for re-fuelling but he would return in ten minutes, no later, most of the passengers alighted, Dorothy and myself included, but al and Theresa remained in their seats. We visited the toilets and tried unsuccessfully, to buy a cup of tea. At 5.55 pm all passengers assembled at the pick-up point.

By now everyone in the coach station was feeling the intense heat! It had been a very hot day in London and the temperature in Victoria was approaching 90 f. By 6.15 pm the younger children in the party were very restless, as was everyone else, and when the coach turned up, at 6.35 pm no one was in the best of moods. The driver offered no apology or explanation. Neither did he get a collection. Albert told us later that after re-fuelling, this oaf decided to wash down the coach!

After what seemed to be several unnecessary detours, we reached Digbeth (Birmingham) at 9.30 pm and our son-in-law Philip was waiting with our car. We walked into our home at 10.00 pm and for the following half-hour teapots and bottles were very much in evidence. Our niece Jenny arrived shortly afterwards and took her parents home, then Philip went home, then Dorothy and I looked at the cups, saucers, plates and glasses, left them exactly where they were and went to bed.

The End of the story

So that was the end of Colin and Dorothy's first visit to Holland and the Niebeeks, and gives an insight to Colin's character and nature. He does not mention much of his ordeal as a prisoner of the Nazi, and nothing about the death march on which so many of his fellow prisoners died. Other than mention that he was interrogated intensively he gives no information of the nature of that interrogation. He was curious to know the name of the traitor, but once known he could forget it with no bitterness that this man had most likely (if the Dutch had returned him safely to England) deprived him of resuming his service in the RAF and becoming a pilot. I do not know the traitor's name but believe the Dutch resistance would have dealt with him.

I am not sure if Colin knew of the extent of Henk Sietsma's activities during the Nazi occupation of Holland, which were considerable. Henk with his brother Hein formed an underground resistance group dedicated to providing places for families and individual Jews to hide, providing food and fake identification papers.

The name of the group was 'Helpt Elkander In Nood' - which translates into English as 'Help each other in need.' Members of this group included Hein's fiancé Berendina (Diet) Eman, as well as the Meervelds and Van Veluws who met Colin on his visit.

Henk and Hein Sietsma were arrested in 1944 and transported to Dachau. Hein's fiancé was arrested and imprisoned for some months in Vught. In October 1944, Hein managed to send a note to his fiancé, folded into a one-centimetre package. He wrote, 'Even if we never meet each other again on this earth, we will never be sorry for what we did. We will never regret that we took this stand, and know, Diet, that of every human being in the world, I loved you the most.'

Hein Sietsma died in Dachau on 21st January 1945, aged 25. Their group saved many Jewish families and individuals as well as British and American aircrew.

It was in 1977 that Yad Vashem, the World Holocaust Remembrance Centre in Jerusalem, recognized Hein and Henk as 'Righteous Among The Nations'. Berendina was later honoured in 1998.

Colin and Dorothy did go back to Holland several times and were invited to an audience with ex-Queen Juliana of the Netherlands and her husband Prince Bernhard at their retirement residence the Soestdijk palace, located in the province of Utrecht. Juliana and her husband lived there until they died in 2004; she had abdicated in April 1980 in favour of her daughter Beatrix, after which she took the title of Her Royal Highness and was very active in charitable causes to well into her 80s.

Left: Hein Sietsma, 4th October 1919 - 21st January 1945. Right: Colin meeting Queen Juliana and Prince Bernhard. Photo by Herman Von Damm.

I believe the event Colin and Dorothy attended was both a celebration and appreciation of the work of the wartime resistance, of which Henk Sietsma was a major participant. Among those invited were many airmen whom his group had assisted when they found themselves in Holland, hence Colin and Dorothy's inclusion.

Remembrance

After the war came recriminations and controversy about the role of Bomber Command in the destruction of more than 50% of all major German cities - in particular the city of Dresden, which was deemed by some of being of no strategic importance and was therefore a war crime. Such comments were an embarrassment to the British government at the end of the war, which resulted in the sacrifices of these brave men being played down except for some of their exceptional actions such as the Dam Buster's raid, which flooded the Ruhr valley.

Bomber Command was largely left out of celebrations of Victory in Europe; no specific Bomber Command medal was issued. Arthur Harris received no peerage or other honour from the post 1945 government. The official British Bombing Survey, completed in 1946, was left unpublished for half a century.

When Harris became Air Chief Marshal of Bomber Command in early 1942 to carry out the British government's policy of attacking German cities and infrastructure, the bomber force had a clear-cut role, which they had not before his appointment. This role saw the 1,000 bomber raids (Colin took part in all three) resulting in Hitler's Minister of Armaments Albert Speer commenting, after the shock of these largest air raids the world had ever seen, that if they continued Germany could not continue the war. They did not continue, however, due to the heavy losses of aircraft and crew depleting the bomber force.

In May 1992, a statue of Arthur Harris was finally unveiled on the Strand in London by the Queen Mother, but to shouts of 'He was a war criminal!' and 'Mass murderer!' The statue was subjected to repeated vandalism and placed under 24 hour guard for some months. What these protesters had not considered was the many millions of deaths the Nazi regime in Germany were responsible for. Nothing could be more evil and vile than the murder of at least six million Jews, just because they were Jews.

The last words on this issue should I believe be left to Arthur Harris, who said after the German bombing of our cities (such as Coventry):

'They sowed the wind, and now they are going to reap the whirlwind.'

It was not until June 2012 that a long overdue memorial to the men of Bomber Command was unveiled by the Queen. It is located in Green Park, along Piccadilly, London; it is made from Portland stone with bronze sculptures of airmen in flying dress.

Notably, both of these memorials were financed by public subscription and not with government funds.

When you travel around this wonderful Great Britain of ours and enjoy the sun glistening on the surface of a lake or are enthralled by the beautiful views of our countryside, just for a moment think of those young men who, at dusk many years ago, climbed into their aircraft knowing for certain that many of them would not see another day. Their survival rate was less than a soldier on the Somme during the First World War. Remember their courage and sacrifice for their country; if you do that then they will never be forgotten. This is the end of this story, but the story of human courage and sacrifice will never end.

The centrepiece of the Bomber Command memorial.
Photograph by Zeisterre. (CC BY-SA 3.0).

Written by John C. Sedgley.
Published in association with West Bromwich Local History Society.
With thanks to: Colin's daughter Linda and her husband Philip;
Brendan Jackson for editing support and guidance.

www.westbromwichhistory.com